The Art of Forecasting Using Diurnal Charts

Sophia Mason

ISBN: 0-86690-330-5
First Printing 1977
Current Printing 1997

Published by:
American Federation of Astrologers, Inc.
PO Box 22040
6535 S. Rural Road
Tempe, Arizona 85285

Printed in the United States of America

Dedication

To Donna Fiorillo

A faithful friend whose
dedication I can never repay.

Books by Sophia Mason

Forecasting With New, Full and Quarter Moons
Basic Fundamentals of the Natal Chart
Aspects Between Signs
Understanding Planetary Placements
Lunations and Predictions
The Art of Forecasting Using Diurnal Charts
Delineation of Progressions
From One House to Another
Aquarian-Cancerian Journal
of Fatal Accidents, Volumes I and II
(by Sophia Mason and Vince Ploscik)
Sexuality
(by Sophia Mason and Vince Ploscik)

Contents

What Is
A Diurnal Chart?

Diurnal charts forecast present events. Some individuals experience difficulty in determining how a transiting planet will operate within the framework of a natal chart. Diurnal charts are the essence of proofreading these transiting aspects.

Main Functions of A Diurnal Chart

- Indicates basic action for the month ahead.
- Forecasts minor incidents and eventful days, and in some cases, major events.
- Serves as a catalyst for timing slow moving transiting planets.
- Proofreader of transiting aspects to natal planets.
- Determines the best times for handling money matters, purchasing lottery tickets, and winning at bingo and games of chance, and the best time to travel, pass school and driving tests, get one's hair done, or apply for a job.

Every year, beginning on the birthday, everyone begins a new evolution through all twelve signs of the zodiac. As can be seen, the natal rising sign does not stand alone, but is merely a part of the whole.

On one's birthday, the diurnal Ascendant is exactly the same as in the natal chart. From that point on, the different effects of each sign as it appears on the diurnal Ascendant are felt: a change of mood, temperament, experiences, and people affecting the sphere of the individual's life.

Other Predictive Techniques

Progressions: Progressions are an excellent source for timing personal events such as marriages, births, or job changes. A progressed planet in aspect to a natal planet is usually in effect for a period of three years: one year while the progressed planet is within one degree orb of applying, another year while exact, and a third year for the one degree orb of separating from the aspect.

Solar Returns: Solar returns are indicative of trends that are most likely to occur during the year ahead. This chart is erected every year on one's birthday for the exact time that the Sun reaches the same degree as the natal Sun. A solar return chart is generally used in collaboration with the natal chart.

New Moons, Full Moons, and Eclipses: These lunations are used as predictive tools to indicate trends and events most likely to occur during the coming month. This is often the major element in setting off progressed aspects occurring in one's chart. They also are effective in activating slow moving transiting planets (Jupiter, Saturn, Uranus, Neptune, and Pluto) in aspect with natal planets. The eclipse position, however, should be watched for at least a year.

Constructing A Diurnal Chart

A diurnal chart is a birth chart for the day in question. It is a one-time transit chart using the same calculations that were used in the erection of the native's natal chart, except the sidereal time for that day is used in place of the natal sidereal time. Be sure to use the same longitude and latitude of birth. Do not alter the natal figures in any way. Do not take Daylight Saving Time into consideration unless it was in effect at the time of birth.

The man used in the example on the next page was born October 12, 1954 in Cleveland, Ohio at 12:14 p.m. Eastern

Standard Time, 81W43, 41N30. The diurnal chart was erected for June 2, 1974.

Setting Up A Diurnal Chart Using A Computer

If you have a computer, you can set up a diurnal chart for as many days in advance as needed. This can be quite handy if you are driving on an interstate highway, for example, as diurnal charts can alert you to possible hazardous driving conditions. If you are planning to visit cities that have casinos, you'll be aware of any potential for winning.

Regardless of which astrological computer program you use, they all pretty much apply the same set-up system. The following examples are for months that have Daylight Savings Time in effect. Notice that with both examples Eastern Standard Time was used even though the diurnal charts were for different months and years with Daylight Savings Time in effect.

	Birth Data	Diurnal Data
Name:	Male	Male
Date:	June 2, 1974	August 1, 1997
Time:	12:14 PM EST	12:14 PM EST
Longitude:	81W43	81W43
Latitude:	41N30	41N30

As you can see, the last three figures are constant for both diurnal charts; only the dates have been changed. It is imperative that you do not alter any of the figures used for your natal chart.

In the advanced astrology class in the Valley Forge High School Adult Education program we experimented with a woman's chart who was born in Paris, France. The ruler of her natal tenth house cusp would soon be squaring the ruler of her natal twelfth house cusp. The diurnal chart that we used for France indicated that her boss would enter the hospital in three days as her natal tenth house ruler would exactly conjunct her diurnal tenth house cusp and at the same time square the ruler of her natal twelfth house. The diurnal chart for Parma, Ohio indicated a hospital entry would be three days earlier. Her boss entered the hospital three days later on the day her diurnal chart for Paris, France had the natal ruler of her tenth house cusp conjunct her diurnal tenth house squaring the ruler of her natal twelfth house cusp. We have conducted countless experiments with students born in different states who are now residing in Parma, Ohio. The result is always the same: The diurnal chart for the birth place is always right on target while the Parma, Ohio chart is off by a few days.

Calculations without A Computer

It is far too difficult to illustrate a diurnal chart that is erected mathematically by hand. There are too many different methods. However, they all have one thing in common—they begin the mathematical calculations with the Sidereal Time. With this in mind all you have to do to set up a diurnal chart by hand is to mentally erase the Sidereal Time you used at birth and replace it with the Sidereal Time for the day for which you wish to set up a diurnal chart.

Do not adjust the transiting Moon according to your birth time. Take the Moon directly out of the ephemeris and continue to add one degree every two hours until the transiting Moon conjuncts an angular house cusp or your natal or diurnal transiting planets. This will provide you with an approximate three-hour span of time during which an event is likely to transpire.

If, for example, we had set up a diurnal chart for August 1, 1997 Daylight Savings Time, the transiting Moon would have been at 18 Cancer at noon in Greenwich, England. The transiting Moon should have been about 18 Cancer at 8:00 a.m. Eastern Daylight Time, at 18 Cancer at 7:00 a.m. Central Standard Time, at 6:00 a.m. Mountain Daylight Time, and 5:00 a.m. Pacific Daylight Time. We would have started with this point and added one degree every two hours until the transiting Moon touched a sensitive point in the diurnal chart.

The Transiting Moon with Computer Charts

A computer chart will always adjust the transiting Moon

according to your time of birth. If, for example, you were born at 3:00 p.m. and the computer has the transiting Moon at 28 Aries, which has already aspected several of your natal or diurnal planets at 25 Leo, to determine the time for this event to take place you will have to subtract one degree from the transiting/diurnal Moon for every two hours. The approximate time for the event to take place would be between 8:00 and 10:00 a.m. Daylight Savings Time, which would be six hours earlier (always allow one degree applying, another exact, and a third separating). If the transiting/diurnal Moon or the planet in question is conjunct an angular house cusp or any house cusp, the event will be more pronounced. For example, if the transiting Moon at 25 Leo conjuncts your ninth house cusp during the early morning hours and at the same time trines a natal or diurnal planet, you may hear surprising news or receive a gift from a distance (ninth house cusp).

The transiting planets are placed inside the diurnal chart with the natal planets around the outside. Do not underestimate the power of semisquares or sesquisquares, as they can touch upon houses that are out of range of squares.

Keep in mind that the transiting/diurnal Sun will be in the same house in which it is positioned in the natal chart. However, if the transiting/diurnal Sun is near a house cusp, it is possible for the transiting Sun in the diurnal chart to be in the next adjoining house. This often occurs whenever signs of long ascension (Cancer, Leo, Virgo, Libra, Scorpio, and Sagittarius) are on the diurnal Ascendant.

General Rules for Interpretation

Charts

Make special note of the fact that the diurnal chart does not operate alone. It must be used in collaboration with the natal chart.

Orbs

Only exact orbs are allowed between planets or to the diurnal house cusps if one is to determine the exact day an event is to take place.

Ascendant

Note the house position of the diurnal Ascendant in the natal chart. This is the area of life that will be brought to the fore during the coming month. For example, if Libra is on the diurnal Ascendant and it is positioned natally on the eighth house cusp, then joint finances will be brought to attention during the ensuing month. Also, house, car, or life insurance; alimony, income tax, mortgage payments, debts, change of plans, and all conditions to do with eighth house matters.

Libra on the diurnal Ascendant tends to draw the native into a month of socializing and parties, or just a strong desire to spend an enjoyable evening in the company of others. This sign rising often accompanies the receipt of wedding invitations or attendance at baby showers. The native seeks peace and harmony during this period of time and may have trouble making decisions.

If either natal or transiting Venus are in the sixth house or receive a difficult aspect from a planet in the diurnal sixth house or its ruler, the native may develop a kidney infection or some other Libra related illness.

Ascendant Ruler

The ruler of the diurnal Ascendant, and its house and sign position in the diurnal chart, reveals the area of life affecting the native's outlook for the month ahead: where the individual will put forth much effort and the areas of life in which the native will be personally motivated to do well at this point.

The ruling planet of the diurnal Ascendant describes the nature of the impact the individual will make upon others, especially those who are governed by the house in which the diurnal Ascendant ruler is posited. The ruler also affects the individual on a physical level, denoting general areas of illness or weakness. All aspects to the ruler should be carefully noted throughout the coming month.

Transiting Planets

Aspects presently occurring in the natal chart between transiting planets or from transiting planets to natal planets can go completely unnoticed unless:

- One of the planets involved happens to be the ruler of the diurnal Ascendant.
- One of the planets involved is positioned in an angular house in the diurnal chart.
- One of the aspecting planets is also aspecting an angular house cusp at the same time.

Otherwise, the occurring aspect will have an effect on someone else and the native may hear about the incident several days later, if at all.

For example, you are more apt to feel the effects of transiting

Mars squaring your natal Venus at the time that you have the signs Aries, Taurus, or Libra rising on the diurnal Ascendant. Otherwise, this aspect can occur with no ill effects whatsoever.

Ruler Changes Signs or Houses

Anytime the ruler of the diurnal Ascendant changes houses or signs during the course of the month, it will immediately alter the native's attitude or circumstances according to its new position. This is especially noticeable with the transiting Sun, Mercury, Venus, or Mars.

First House Aspects

Aspects to natal or transiting planets positioned in the diurnal first house will create activity or circumstances in the native's personal affairs.

Angular House Cusps

The angular house cusps (first, fourth, seventh, and tenth) also are important. Aspects to these house cusps or planets therein will promote general activity according to their natal house positions.

Dormant Planets

Diurnal charts activate dormant natal and transiting planets. For example, transiting Uranus is positioned in one's fourth house for a period of seven years. The native accidentally locks himself out of his home and has to break open the front door to get in. There were no aspects presently operating from either natal or transiting planets to Uranus in the fourth house. However, in the diurnal chart, Uranus was squaring the diurnal Ascendant and the unexpected occurred in the home (transiting Uranus positioned in the natal fourth house). The energy of Uranus is unexpected and because of this there will be unexpected incidents occurring in the home from time to time. Diurnal charts are like timing devices and will set off the energy of slow moving transiting planets with no visible aspects in the natal chart.

Planets in Houses

Planets in the diurnal houses show the kind of energy that is now taking place, revealing what and where it is happening as well as who might be involved. The houses they rule reveal why it is happening and who might be the cause of it. A planet positioned in a house is stronger than the one it rules and therefore should be given first consideration.

Planets

Planets in the diurnal chart represent behavior, attitudes, activities, and conditions expressed and encountered. Their sign positions represent attitudes and, hence, modification of behavior expressed by the planets. The house position denotes the area of life in which the behavior is expressed (by planets) and to which the attitude applies (by sign).

Timing of Planets in Houses

The average length of time that each planet (transiting or natal) will be positioned in one house is approximately thirty days, except for retrograde planets and the transiting Sun, Venus, and Mercury, which tend to huddle quite close to the houses they occupied at birth. The houses the transiting Sun, Venus, and Mercury rule in the diurnal chart, plus the signs they occupy during any one particular month will be of paramount importance, especially if either one is the ruler of the diurnal Ascendant for that month.

Heavily Occupied Houses

Special attention should be given to houses heavily occupied by natal and transiting planets. A preponderance of planets (natal or transiting) in one house emphasizes the area of life requiring special handling at that time.

Transiting Moon

The transiting Moon (unlike the natal or transiting planets) will transit through all twelve houses every month, with a different sign rising each month. Activities in one's personal affairs tend to increase and undergo frequent changes when signs of short ascension are rising (Capricorn, Aquarius, Pisces, Aries, Taurus, and Gemini). This is due to the fact that the transiting Moon will

10

move at a faster pace through each house. Note in the tables of houses how a house cusp will skip a degree when signs of short ascension are on the Ascendant.

Finding the Diurnal Ascendant

Once the sidereal time is determined for the day in question (whether you calculate by hand or with a computer), use the latitude of birth from the tables of houses to find the present diurnal rising sign. Each line of the rising sign in the tables of houses is equivalent to one day. Count down to see how many days it will be rising, which can vary from six to forty-seven days, depending upon the latitude.

Signs of short ascension (Capricorn, Aquarius, Pisces, Aries, Taurus, and Gemini) tend to move rather quickly over the Ascendant; therefore, affairs and activities undergo a vast turnover. Look at your natal chart and note the houses containing these signs of short ascension. These areas of life move at a faster pace and seem to require less attention.

Signs of long ascension (Cancer, Leo, Virgo, Libra, Scorpio, and Sagittarius) move at a slower rate. The affairs of these houses in your natal chart demand more attention, and more problems are created or gains made because you are involved with the affairs of these houses for a longer period of time.

Knowing how many days a particular sign will be rising will determine how many days a planet will be the ruler of the diurnal Ascendant. If, for example, on September 3 of any year, the diurnal rising sign changes from twenty-nine degrees Pisces to zero degrees Aries at 41 degrees latitude, it will be immediately obvious that the planet Mars will be the ruler of the diurnal Ascendant for the next eighteen days. All aspects to Mars will denote days of special attention. The house and sign position of transiting Mars in the diurnal chat will denote what kind of activity will take place. Even if a daily diurnal chart is not used, there is the advantage of knowing which planet rules the diurnal Ascendant and for how many days, as well as the areas of life being brought to attention.

Same Sign Rising

The diurnal chart will have the same Ascendant at the same time every year of the native's life. It is the changing positions of the transiting planets that denote changes in the area of life in which the diurnal Ascendant is located (natal house).

For example, someone with a Scorpio Sun and Sagittarius on the natal Ascendant will have Sagittarius rising on the diurnal chart beginning from his birthday and continuing for the next thirty days or so. Then, around Thanksgiving, his diurnal Ascendant changes to Capricorn and every year, about this time, he wonders why he becomes so easily depressed at holiday time. He may regard the holidays as more work than they are worth, or as a heavy responsibility that falls on his shoulders every year.

Suppose transiting Saturn, ruler of the diurnal Ascendant, was in Virgo, the sign on the diurnal ninth house cusp. It is almost sure that in-laws or those living at a distance will be a source of concern or a problem (Saturn) during the holidays.

Frequency of Diurnal Charts

Is it necessary to erect a diurnal chart every day? In the beginning, yes, for it is a great teacher in helping one determine how the energies of each planet will manifest through various aspects, houses, and signs. Setting up daily diurnal charts will help the student learn to better read them, and they also are a valuable tool for proofreading the areas in which transiting planets in aspect to natal planets will operate.

Lunations

Diurnal charts erected at the time of the new Moon, full Moon, and quarter Moon will offer feedback on what to expect from these lunations. Although transiting Sun, Mercury, and Venus will huddle quite close to the house they were positioned in at birth, they nevertheless will be in different signs and rule different houses in the diurnal chart.

Natal and Diurnal House Cusps

Learn to combine the diurnal house cusp position with the natal house cusp position. For example, a transiting or natal planet conjuncts the diurnal second house cusp with the sign Aries on it. Because Aries is on the tenth house cusp of the natal chart, money matters to do with the career, boss, or parents will be activated.

The kind of energy depends on the planet conjuncting the second house cusp and the house it rules in either the natal or diurnal chart. Look also to the condition of transiting Mars and its house and sign position to determine why the link between money and tenth house matters is developing, or the cause of it and who may be involved.

Planets positioned in the second house, whether they are transiting or natal planets, also will become important because its house cusp has been activated by a planet conjunct it. Are there any aspects to these planets in the diurnal second house and what houses do they rule in the diurnal chart? View these planets in the second house as affecting the financial area of life through tenth house matters (the sign Aries is on the diurnal second house cusp and is natally positioned on the tenth house cusp).

Planets and Angular Houses

Planets in aspect to angular house cusps or to planets positioned in angular houses (first, fourth, seventh, and tenth) generally bring matters to immediate attention. Planets in aspect to house cusps or to planets that are not angular often concern the affairs of others and do not manifest themselves immediately. Thus, the native may not hear of an incident for several days, if at all. Unless the planet in question is the ruler of the diurnal Ascendant, then the action will be felt but more likely through friends or someone within the immediate family circle.

Neptune and Pisces

The energy of Neptune and Pisces is elusive. When Neptune aspects or conjuncts any house cusp, angular or otherwise, the matter is usually hidden. This factor can cause a delay in action, even with an angular house cusp or when Neptune is aspecting an angular planet.

Aspects to the Diurnal Ascendant

Aspects to the diurnal Ascendant help determine favorable or unfavorable days for handling personal affairs and for dealing with certain individuals or situations.

The transiting Sun, Venus, and Mercury in the diurnal chart will always be in or close to the same house position they held at birth. In many cases, it may be impossible for the transiting Sun, Venus, or Mercury to aspect the diurnal Ascendant.

However, the natal Sun, Venus, and Mercury will enter all twelve houses of the diurnal chart during the year. They will sextile and trine the diurnal Ascendant twice, and conjunct it once. The natal Sun, Venus, and Mercury will square the diurnal Ascendant twice and oppose it once.

Only exact orbs are used. Always refer to the natal chart to determine the house position being brought to attention. For example, if transiting Jupiter is going through the natal fifth house and is trining the diurnal Ascendant, this can be one of the best days for gambling, buying a lottery ticket, or playing bingo. General suggestions are given for each planet, and in time you will see how they operate within the framework of your own chart.

Sun

The Sun represents one's ego, sense of pride, and self-confidence; vitality and general physical condition; plans for the future that may affect one's position in life; dealings with men in general, one's father, boss, or someone who holds a position of authority; the husband in a woman's chart; conditions surrounding children, romance, sporting events, gambling, bingo games, purchase of lottery or raffle tickets; and invitations to the theater or dinner.

Sun (natal and transiting) favorably aspecting the diurnal Ascendant: This brings ease in dealing with men. If you, your husband, or child are participating in a sporting event (bowling, hockey, basketball, football, etc.), the chances of winning are excellent. All matters listed under the Sun are now favored.

Sun unfavorably aspecting the diurnal Ascendant: Wait for another day if you must deal with men, bosses, or those in authority. They may be opposed to your ideas or suggestions. A child's team may lose a football game or a teacher call to discuss the child's behavior in school. Your vitality is down and you may feel listless.

Sun conjunct the Ascendant: If it is the natal Sun, it will bring the affairs of its natal house and sign position to the attention of the native. As an example, consider a native with natal Sun in the third house in Sagittarius. On the day the natal Sun conjuncts the diurnal Ascendant, the native may receive communication from a close relative (generally a man) or from someone who lives at a distance; there is also the possibility of legal affairs being brought to attention.

Much of the activity is determined by any transiting planets making close aspects to the natal Sun. If the transiting Sun is conjunct the diurnal Ascendant (this may happen quite often if the individual was born close to 6:00 a.m.), the natal house being transited by the Sun is brought to attention. Should the natal or transiting Sun conjunct the seventh house cusp, then the affairs of the Sun's position in the natal chart will concern other people or activity will occur as a result of other individuals.

Moon

The Moon represents moods, sensitivity and emotional responses; the stomach and an emotional desire to eat; the home and parent; women in general, usually mature women, married women or those who have a child (mothers); changing conditions; general public; and a sense of security and how the public sees the native.

Moon (natal or transiting) favorably aspecting the Diurnal Ascendant: This is the best time to deal with the general public and women. There is emotional stability and the capacity to handle changing conditions.

Moon unfavorably aspecting the diurnal Ascendant: This can bring trouble through or with women. There is emotional instability through upsetting conditions or the immediate environment, and it is a time of low vitality.

Moon conjunct the Ascendant: If it is the natal Moon, it will bring the affairs of its natal house and sign position to the attention of the native. The emotions are generally aroused or the native is touched by the thoughtfulness of another individual. However, this could be an emotionally upsetting day if the natal Moon is receiving an adverse aspect from a transiting planet at the time of the conjunction.

The transiting Moon in conjunction with the diurnal Ascendant brings to attention the affairs of the natal house through which it is transiting. Try to determine the time this conjunction will take place.

For example, if the diurnal Ascendant is seventeen degrees Sagittarius and the transiting Moon is listed in the noon ephemeris for that day at sixteen degrees Sagittarius, the transiting Moon will conjunct the diurnal Ascendant at approximately 9:00 a.m. if the city of residence is five hours (Central Standard Time) earlier than Universal Time (Greenwich Mean Time). This is because the Moon moves approximately one degree every two hours, and the noon Universal Time position of the Moon is equivalent to 7:00 a.m. Central Standard Time.

At approximately 9:00 a.m. when the transiting Moon conjuncts the diurnal Ascendant, the native will be involved in an activity concerning travel or communication from a distance according to the natal house position of the transiting Moon. If conjunct the diurnal seventh house cusp, the Moon will bring emotional responses through the affairs of others.

Venus

Venus represents gifts, invitations, and social gatherings; romance, affection, and the desire to spend the evening with someone; physical appearance, hair style, clothes, and jewelry or articles of artistic quality; women in general and, as a rule, younger women or those one may consider attractive.

Venus (natal or transiting) favorably aspecting the diurnal Ascendant: This is an excellent time for purchasing new clothing or having one's hair styled and cut. A man might meet a new woman or have a date with one. A gift or invitation is possible.

Venus unfavorably aspecting the diurnal Ascendant: This is not a good time for planning social affairs. There is trouble with or through women. If one goes to a hair stylist, the cut may be too short or the style wrong. As there is indecisiveness in making purchases, this is not a time to shop for clothes as the native will not find what he or she is looking for.

Venus conjunct the Ascendant: If it is natal Venus, it will bring the affairs of its natal house and sign position to the attention of the native. Gifts and invitations are possible, and if natally positioned in the sixth house, they may come from co-workers. If natal Venus is in the fifth house, the affairs of a female child or school matters are brought to attention.

Transiting Venus conjunct the diurnal Ascendant brings to attention the affairs of the natal house through which it is transiting. If transiting through the twelfth house, for example, the native may learn of a secret female enemy or a female may be in the hospital, depending upon the aspects transiting Venus makes to natal transiting planets at the time of the conjunction.

Venus conjunct the seventh house cusp brings about a desire to be in the company of others through social affairs. Again, gifts or invitations are possible.

Mercury

Mercury represents conversing with others; news, communication, correspondence, writing letters, or signing documents; mental pursuits, the ability to comprehend written material; a busy time taking care of small details and running errands; matters to do with brothers, sisters, cousins, neighbors, or younger people; books and school or office supplies.

Mercury (natal or transiting) favorably aspecting the diurnal Ascendant: This is a good time for taking tests, handling necessary details, writing letters, making phone calls, signing papers, and taking short trips.

Mercury (natal or transiting) unfavorably aspecting the diurnal Ascendant: This may bring problems with neighbors or upsetting news or letters. Someone may ask a favor of the native, adding more burdens to what he or she feels is already a busy day ahead. Mental errors are possible, as is high nervous tension.

Mercury conjunct the Ascendant: If it is natal Mercury, it will bring about communication through phone calls or letters in accordance with its natal house and sign position. This can stimulate the mind or scatter the energy into a variety of projects.

Transiting Mercury conjunct the diurnal Ascendant brings to attention the affairs of the natal house through which it is transiting. If Mercury is in Sagittarius for example, on the day of the conjunction the native may make or receive long distance phone calls or letters from a distance. Whether it brings favorable results depends upon the aspects transiting Mercury makes to natal or transiting planets at the time of the conjunction.

Mercury conjunct the seventh house cusp can bring communication concerning the affairs of others according to the natal house position.

Mars

Mars represents activity, energy, impatience, impulsiveness, and the desire for wanting something now; competitiveness in sports; arguments; mechanical inclination; standing up for one's principles; sexual or physical stimulation; and male influence or dealings with assertive or aggressive men.

Mars (natal or transiting) favorably aspecting the diurnal Ascendant: This endows the necessary energy for tackling projects. There is success in sports, recreation, and competitive matters, and a high degree of sexuality. There may be favors from men in the military or police force. It is a good time to go to the dentist, and buy a new car or have one repaired. Anything that requires excessive output of energy, such as heavy house or garage cleaning, yard work, and washing cars, is favored.

Mars (natal or transiting) unfavorably aspecting the diurnal Ascendant: This causes impatience with others. It could lead to accidents or arguments, car trouble, or traffic tickets. There may be a feverish condition or trouble with the sinuses. This aspect is often accompanied with nervous, intense energy and a desire to lash out at someone for no apparent reason.

Mars conjunct the Ascendant: If it is natal Mars, it may create the tendency to become argumentative or cause slight accidents according to its natal house and sign position. If natal Mars is positioned in the natal sixth house, for example, there may be slight accidents in relation to work conditions such as spilling coffee on office papers or dropping a wrench on one's foot.

Transiting Mars conjunct the diurnal Ascendant brings to attention the affairs of the natal house through which Mars is transiting. If adversely afflicted at the time Mars conjuncts the diurnal Ascendant, that particular day will require patience with others to avoid possible friction or arguments. It is a day to protect against the possibility of accidents.

When Mars is conjunct the diurnal seventh house cusp, other individuals may be opposed to the native's ideas, and arguments or friction can result through their impatience with the native.

Jupiter

Jupiter represents good luck, a feeling of optimism, opportunities for expansion in one's job or through mental, material, and social pursuits; a desire for travel or to communicate with those at a distance; higher learning such as college or adult education classes, legal matters or dealings with law enforcement agencies; and brothers- or sisters-in-law and their affairs.

Jupiter (natal or transiting) favorably aspecting the diurnal Ascendant: This is a good time for travel. There may be communication from those at a distance, and legal affairs may become activated if indicated in the natal chart. The native may take an exam, or communicate on a large scale through radio or television appearances.

Jupiter (natal or transiting) unfavorably aspecting the diurnal Ascendant: This is not a good time for pursuing legal activity, or for signing legal documents. Opportunities are hindered or hit a snag. The native may receive a low score on an exam. In-laws may be a source of irritation.

Jupiter conjunct the diurnal Ascendant: If it is natal Jupiter, it can be beneficial and produce success or gain according to the affairs of the natal house and sign position. However, if afflicted by transiting planets at the time of the conjunction it can bring about disturbing news from a distance, court action, or a traffic ticket. Transiting Jupiter can indicate gain or success according the natal house through which it is transiting. Generally, it is a day in which the native decides to take legal action, makes or receives long distance phone calls, or letters arrive from a distance. If the native ordered a package from another state, it can bring about the delivery.

Jupiter conjunct the seventh house cusp can bring benefits or opposition through others. If there is an adverse aspect to Jupiter on the day of the conjunction, the native's appointment is canceled, a trip is delayed, or he or she won't see eye to eye with individuals ruled by the natal house and sign position.

Saturn

Saturn represents duties, responsibilities, hindrances, delays, and restrictions; one's sense of obligation to job, boss, or family; ambition and desire to achieve prestige or public recognition; needed discipline and restraint to complete tasks; older people, those in authority, a parent or grandparent, and city officials; someone from the past; a person who uses another for personal gain or attainment; and an end to an old matter.

Saturn (natal or transiting) favorably aspecting the diurnal Ascendant: This gives good logic, organizational ability, and concentration. It is an excellent time for seeking favors from those in authority. Long range goals may be realized or come to completion. The native may meet or hear from an old friend, and the job or career takes a turn for the better.

Saturn (natal or transiting) unfavorably aspecting the diurnal Ascendant: This is a time when the native feels physically down and tired, inadequate, inhibited, fearful, depressed, and burdened with responsibilities. Quite often, this feeling of restriction is self-imposed, with the native feeling as though nothing worthwhile is being achieved in life. It is not the ideal day to begin new projects, because there will be delays. It is a time to lay low and conserve energy. There may be achy knees or problems with teeth or dentures.

Saturn conjunct the Ascendant: If it is natal Saturn, it may bring restrictions, cause delays and concerns, or added responsibilities through the affairs of the natal house and sign in which it is positioned. Much, of course, depends upon the aspects it receives from transiting planets. It can be a productive day in which the native gains perseverance to finish a task. Many individuals suddenly get the urge to clean the attic or basement on the day Saturn conjuncts the diurnal Ascendant.

Transiting Saturn conjunct the diurnal Ascendant brings to attention the affairs of the natal house through which Saturn is transiting. If unfavorably aspected, this can be a day of depression, a time to lay low and conserve energy.

If Saturn is conjunct the seventh house cusp, older individuals or those in authority may cause restrictions or delays, or be a source of added responsibility according to the affairs of the natal house position.

Uranus

Uranus represents freedom and independence; a desire to do something different and out of the ordinary; forming of new friendships or joining clubs and organizations; an air of excitement bringing unexpected events; a rebellious attitude; an inventive mind; communication or social gatherings with friends; and astrology, electrical appliances, gadgets, auto parts, radio, and television.

Uranus (natal or transiting) favorably aspecting the diurnal Ascendant: This brings unexpected events, which could be in the form of unexpected news, bumping into friends in a restaurant, or winning a lottery prize. The tone of the diurnal chart on the day that natal or transiting Uranus favors the Ascendant should offer some clue as to what kind of event is most likely to occur.

Uranus (natal or transiting) unfavorably aspecting the diurnal Ascendant: This may bring unexpected problems with the car (usually something to do with the electrical system such as the battery) or unexpected trouble with electrical appliances. It is not the day for installing electrical wiring in the home or garage. Check the natal and diurnal charts to determine what the unexpected event might be. The native should not purchase electrical appliances or televisions at this time as there may be repeated problems with them.

Uranus conjunct the Ascendant: The native should expect the unexpected and to be either overjoyed or terribly upset according to the aspects natal Uranus receives from transiting planets that affect the affairs of its natal house and sign position. Transiting Uranus can be exciting or disturbing according to the aspects Uranus receives or makes on the day of the conjunction. Look to the natal house it is transiting to determine what affairs will be brought into action in the most unexpected manner.

Uranus conjunct the seventh house cusp brings unexpected events through the affairs of others according to its natal or transiting position in the natal chart.

Neptune

Neptune represents desire for peace, harmony and seclusion; strong intuitive ability; imagination; psychic experiences, spiritual responses, and meditation; need for escapism through daydreaming or sleeping longer hours than needed; alcoholic beverages, drugs, and medication; music, dancing, writing, or reading poetry; artistic pursuits such as painting, cake decorating, music or dancing lessons; hidden matters, secret enemies, deception, or confusion; hospitals and places of confinement; detective work or behind-the-scenes activities; and faith and trust in others.

Neptune (natal or transiting) favorably aspecting the diurnal Ascendant: This is a good day for visiting a psychic or getting together with those who have mediumistic ability, or beginning belly dancing or music lessons. Meditation brings peace of mind and perhaps a solution to a problem that has been harbored in the back of the native's mind. There can be unusual events or psychic experiences. If possible, the native should go dancing or take time out for listening to music. This position favors police activity, and a gift may be received that is hand made or of some unusual artistic quality.

Neptune (natal or transiting) unfavorably aspecting the diurnal Ascendant: This can cause possible withdrawal from normal daily activities due to a sense of self-pity. There may be deception through others, an imposition from another, or a confused state of mind. Someone may be keeping a secret from the native and he or she should be aware that something may be going on behind his or her back. One tends to sleep more than usual or overindulge in alcoholic beverages. There may be news of someone in the hospital, detection of secret enemies, or a moody or temperamental nature. This is not the day for making logical decisions.

Neptune (natal or transiting) conjunct the Ascendant: This is a day of confusion, chaos or the desire to seek seclusion. If one has a low resistance to alcohol, a drinking binge may result. There may be news of someone entering the hospital.

If natal Neptune is conjunct the diurnal Ascendant, the confusing condition may be centered around the affairs of its natal house and sign position. Much, of course, depends upon the aspects that natal Neptune receives from transiting planets. It is possible to receive a beautiful, hand made gift or volunteer for a charitable organization.

It transiting Neptune conjuncts the diurnal Ascendant, note what natal house Neptune is transiting, as these are the affairs that will require compassion, sympathy, or understanding. If Neptune conjuncts the seventh house cusp, secret enemies come into the open. Someone outside the immediate circle may enter the hospital, or the native may hear gossip and rumors about such a person.

Again, what is the natal house position of either transiting or natal Neptune? What are the aspects to natal or transiting Neptune? All these conditions are important in determining who, what and why Neptune is affecting the native on that particular day.

Pluto

Pluto represents a change of plans or existing conditions; the desire to change one's hair style, coloring, or personal appearance through diet or manner of dress; discovering that which is hidden or unknown; elimination of material things which are no longer useful; highly tensed state; obsessive feeling to do something; control over others through manipulation or by being in a position to have someone hired or fired; money belonging to others such as joint finances, loans, mortgage and credit payments, alimony or the IRS; matters pertaining to life, car, or homeowners insurance; news of a birth or death; arousal of sexual instincts; and a feeling of revenge.

Pluto (natal or transiting) favorably aspecting the diurnal Ascendant: This is a good day to file an income tax return. The native may receive news about a lowered insurance premium or receive a refund check because of overpayment of a bill or through an error in a checking account. A change of plans occurs, but it turns out for the better. It is a good time to hold a garage sale and eliminate items which are no longer needed, as well as to win a lottery or raffle prize.

Pluto (natal or transiting) unfavorably aspecting the diurnal Ascendant: This may cause one to become angry or tense over some change in plans. Forgotten bills become due, and there may be an increase in insurance premiums. The native may receive news of someone's death. (Usually it is someone outside the native's immediate circle such as a distant friend or cousin. Anyone closer requires verification through the native's progressed chart and the heavier transits or an eclipse.)

Pluto (natal or transiting) conjunct the diurnal Ascendant: If it is natal Pluto, consider its natal house and sign position to determine the source of the change in plans that will affect the native's day for good or bad depending on the aspects received. This can be a day on which joint finances or other people's money will need handling or attention. If it is transiting Pluto, look to the natal house it is transiting. Does Pluto make any aspects to natal planets? Which ones? Does transiting Pluto receive any aspects from transiting planets on the day of the conjunction? Which ones?

Since Pluto rules change and other people's money, generally on the day it conjuncts the diurnal Ascendant the native receives a past due bill or an increase in insurance premiums.

Pluto conjunct the seventh house cusp brings a change of plans resulting through the actions of others.

Rising Signs on the Diurnal Ascendant

Aries

Even though Aries moves so quickly over the eastern horizon, its presence seldom goes unnoticed when rising on the diurnal Ascendant. There is a marked degree of energy and activity. Projects are often initiated at this time or a new venture undertaken. One's attitude becomes impatient, impulsive, and impetuous, leading to possible accidents or arguments. An automobile or other mechanical device may need repairs.

Aries is strongly masculine and therefore generates its energy around the affairs of a male figure in the immediate circle. The clue to this male image and who he might be lies in the diurnal house and sign position at the time Aries is rising. Look also to the natal house that holds Aries for further verification. The Lunation and its aspects to natal and transiting planets offer still another source of determining who the gentleman is that is being brought to attention at this time.

Look at the natal chart. What house has Aries positioned on the cusp (or in the house in the case of intercepted signs). All planets therein, whether they are natal or transiting, will require special handling because they are now positioned in the diurnal first house.

Check the condition of transiting and natal Mars (ruler of Aries) and also progressed Mars, which may have been activated by a slow moving transit, the lunation or an eclipse.

The native should take care of his or her health, as Aries is prone to infections, inflammations, headaches, fevers, sharp pains, surgery, and burns or cuts.

Transiting or natal Mars positioned in the diurnal first house will have the same effect as Aries on the diurnal Ascendant.

Taurus

After the energetic sign Aries has left the diurnal Ascendant, one is ready for a well-deserved rest and the lazy streak of Taurus takes over. The native may self-indulge with the purchase of new clothing or jewelry, but at least will feel more composed and relaxed in comparison to the previous weeks. The power of concentration is good for tackling projects that require meticulous attention. It is a good time to balance the checkbook and pay bills for there is motivation for handling monetary and material possessions. Although one tends to be more cautious with Taurus on the diurnal Ascendant, it is important to watch the purse strings when Venus (ruler of Taurus) is afflicted. It is a time to receive and give gifts.

Who will the native spend money on? Who will be a source of monetary or material drain or gain is shown by the natal house position of the sign Taurus and planets therein.

Check the condition of transiting and natal Venus along with progressed Venus if it has been activated by a slow transit or lunation. Do not be fooled and easily led by Taurus: Peace and harmony may be its prime motivation, however it is ruled by the bull and therefore can produce far more violence than Aries.

Do not overindulge in food, and guard against throat infections.

Transiting or natal Venus positioned in the diurnal first house will have the same effect as Taurus on the diurnal Ascendant.

Gemini

The calming period and the experience of a little relaxation is over. Now the native is getting bored, restless, and ambitious. It is time to communicate, make phone calls, write letters, visit, and get into the swing of things. However, it's important not to become sidetracked by taking on too many projects. The nervous system is riding high but it may get the best of one. There may be some involvement with the affairs of brothers, sisters, cousins, neighbors, or close relations. Now is a good time to advertise, enroll in classes, or take a driving test. One's power of perception is excellent and knowledge is easily acquired as long as he or she doesn't become lost in petty details or waste time with matters that tend only to consume time and energy.

Gemini's natal house position indicates for whom he or she will be driving or doing errands, or visiting or communicating with.

Check the condition of transiting and natal Mercury (ruler of Gemini) and use progressed Mercury only if has been activated by a slow transit or lunation aspect.

Transiting or natal Mercury positioned in the diurnal first house can have the same effect as Gemini on the diurnal Ascendant.

Cancer

The native has communicated with close relatives; now is the time to talk with mom. Not only does one have contacts with a parent, but older women, married women, or young women who are mothers seem to demand much time and energy. Maternal instincts are rather strong, including wanting to bake a cake for someone or invite others for dinner. Someone invites the native out or, if a man, he frequents the better restaurants with someone who enjoys dining out. Matters to do with property or the home may require attention. One feels like cleaning the house, watering the plants, buying new furniture, or redecorating. This can be an emotionally trying time as moods fluctuate from day to day. Not only are temperamental moods experienced, but activities undergo constant changes. This is understandable as the transiting Moon (ruler of Cancer) will be changing houses and signs frequently during the course of the month.

The natal house position of Cancer determines with whom the native becomes emotionally involved and what vein of activity demands so much time in the home.

Check the condition of the transiting and natal Moon along with the progressed Moon if it too has been activated by a slow transit or lunation. A parent or matters to do with the home need attention and should be taken care of at this time.

Fluctuating moods and extreme sensitivity can drive one to eat and cause an increase in weight. Watch the diet and water intake during this month.

Transiting or natal Moon positioned in the diurnal first house can have the same effect as Cancer on the diurnal Ascendant.

Leo

The past month has been emotionally trying, but now the native is beginning to feel a bit more optimistic, ambitious, and hopeful that the future is going to perk up. Children, even if not the native's own, will be a prime concern and this can be an exceptionally busy time in handling their affairs. The native attends PTA meetings, works with scouts, makes costumes for the school play or Halloween, or the school counselor calls. If the native has no children, does not teach school, and is not involved with the affairs of children, it is possible to enroll in school to enhance or further the education. He or she may seek a school counselor or someone who can help select the proper course.

Romance comes into view if one is available. Sporting events are attended or the bowling league joined, for example. Investments come up for renewal. The native feels like entertaining. If the natal or transiting Sun is heavily afflicted, this is the time one is most likely to hear of someone having a heart attack.

The activity that takes place concerning children or schools can be determined by the natal house position of Leo.

Check the condition of the transiting and natal Sun along with the progressed Sun if it too has been activated by a slow transit or lunation.

If weather conditions are changing at the time Leo is on the diurnal Ascendant, take care that windy days do not blow particles into the eyes. This is the time of year when eyes are most likely to tear or water easily. A slight eye infection may occur. Anything more serious, such as a heart attack or back surgery, would require information through progressions, heavy transits to natal planets or an afflicted eclipse position.

Transiting or natal Sun positioned in the diurnal first house can have the same effect as Leo on the diurnal Ascendant. (Individuals born in the early morning hours nearly always have the transiting Sun in the first house of the diurnal chart; therefore, the natal Sun's position in the first house, rather than the transiting Sun, is more likely to produce the above effects.)

Virgo

This is one of the best times to go on a diet; the native becomes aware that he or she has been putting on weight and wants to do something about it. A decision may be made to experiment with health foods, purchase vitamins, or join a health spa. New diet recipes and exercise instructions are clipped out of magazines. One instinctively feels it is time to make an appointment with a physician for a health check-up. Most individuals do this intuitively, without realizing Virgo is on the diurnal Ascendant.

The mind is more analytical, assimilative and detail-minded than ever before. This is the best time for handling tedious tasks that would otherwise drive one up the wall.

If there have been problems with a co-worker or with certain aspects of work details, Virgo on the diurnal Ascendant is more likely to bring it all to a head. If job changes are desired, check the condition of Mercury (ruler of Virgo). This also applies if asking for a raise.

Small pets, aunts and uncles, service repairmen (appliances, plumbing, electrical, etc.), co-workers, tenants, or a pharmacist may require special attention.

Striving for perfection in details can play havoc with the nervous system and intestines, resulting in bowel disorders. Psoriasis or skin eruptions often occur at this time. Health problems with domestic pets may require a visit to the veterinarian.

Additional insight can be gained from checking the natal house position of Virgo.

Check the condition of transiting and natal Mercury along with progressed Mercury if it too has been activated by a slow transit or lunation.

Transiting or natal Mercury positioned in the diurnal first house can have the same effect as Virgo on the diurnal Ascendant.

Libra

The native suddenly feels the need for socializing and being in the company of others with whom he or she has rapport. The affairs of business or marriage partners, those with whom there is a close relationship, such as friends, associates, and the romantic partner, all come to light.

The native may be in a position that calls for dealing with large organizations, corporations, or businesses. If there are problems within the marriage, one may seek the advice of an attorney or marriage counselor. Litigation is sometimes activated with Libra rising. Legal documents may be signed or divorce proceedings started. Announcements of engagements or marriages are received. One gets in the mood for a new hair style and the purchase of new clothes, jewelry, and luxury items.

Energy seems to fluctuate. Arguments are upsetting and the native is in the role of mediator. It can be a month of social activity unless the natal seventh house shows stress in relationships with others; then that matter will have to be dealt with. Circumstances may arise in which the native collaborates with another individual in handling certain matters.

The manner in which circumstances surrounding other people are handled is determined by the natal house position of Libra.

Check the condition of transiting and natal Venus (ruler of Libra) along with progressed Venus if it, too, has been activated by a slow transit or lunation. (Because Venus, Mercury, and the Sun often will appear in the diurnal first house if the individual is born in the early morning hours, more importance should be placed on natal Venus, Mercury, and the Sun when they reach the diurnal first house.)

The native should drink more fluids during this period in order to create a balance within the system and thereby avoid kidney or bladder problems.

Transiting or natal Venus positioned in the diurnal first house can have the same effect as Libra on the diurnal Ascendant.

Scorpio

At this time the native will have the ability and determination to make desired personal changes or overcome bad habits. Now is the time to tackle those jobs that have been put off because they were difficult or disagreeable.

The native will feel a bit withdrawn and secretive during this period of time. A defensive attitude may prevail.

One will have to contend with matters dealing with joint finances (the mate's) or other people's money such as car payments, mortgages, credit cards, alimony, income tax, or insurance premiums. The native either increases life insurance or makes basic changes within the framework of auto or homeowners insurance. Someone may pick this time to discuss the handling of wills and estates.

People insist, much to the native's annoyance, on relaying the finer details of operations or labor pains in child delivery. Death notices of friends, neighbors, or physicians appear in the newspaper. The native may visit a cemetery or attend a funeral. In some way he or she may become involved with matters of the dead, discussions, or holding a seance. A movie on life after death is viewed or a book on the occult or the unknown is purchased. Television shows on reincarnation hold the native's interest.

This can be a fascinating month of deep, intense feelings and a high degree of sexuality. If anyone insults the native or hurts his or her feelings in any way, he or she won't get mad, but will get even.

The natal house position of Scorpio should reveal in what manner joint finances, the occult or personal changes will occur.

Check the condition of transiting and natal Pluto (co-ruler of Scorpio).

The native will feel uptight this month, and should drink a lot of fruit juices and take time out for proper elimination to avoid constipation.

Transiting or natal Pluto positioned in the diurnal first house can have the same effect as Scorpio on the diurnal Ascendant.

Sagittarius

The native receives or makes long distance phone calls. Travel is intriguing; if no trips are made, then plans are made for an upcoming vacation. Many individuals decide to return to college or enroll in adult education evening classes.

Purchases from out-of-state catalogs may be received now. It is a period of time when matters at a distance require handling or attention. If there is legal or court action pending, it may be settled at this time. The affairs of a brother- or sister-in-law and those residing at a distance are activated at this time. The native may take up a new sport such as tennis, racquetball or golf, or purchase an exercise bicycle.

Because Sagittarius rules communication on a large scale, many individuals have their pictures in the paper or appear on radio or television at this time, and may mail publications or brochures to out-of-state patrons. Strangers come into one's life, and they either become friends or are dropped according to the aspects to Jupiter (ruler of Sagittarius) or the conditioning of the diurnal ninth house. A religious spirit prevails and many individuals decide to attend church services or confession.

The native feels optimistic, independent, expansive, and full of good humor. If the aspects to Jupiter are good, the native should listen to intuition and hunches as they could hold the key to a successful enterprise developing in the near future.

The natal house position of Sagittarius should reveal how matters at a distance or relatives of one's mate will affect the native.

Check the condition of transiting and natal Jupiter (ruler of

Sagittarius) along with progressed Jupiter if it too has been activated by a slow transit or lunation.

The native's expansive mood causes overindulgence in food or drink, thereby causing weight gain before the month is over.

Transiting or natal Jupiter positioned in the diurnal first house can produce the same effect as Sagittarius on the diurnal Ascendant.

Capricorn

The native's expansive mood from the previous month gives way to pessimism, feeling down, and depressed. Nothing seems to be going right. No matter what is attempted, there appears to be a drawback. One foot is put forward and two back with the feeling that the fullest potential is not being achieved.

Responsibilities (often self-inflicted) tend to lay heavily and hold one back from what is important in life. The native feels lonely and that no one loves or cares about him or her. Thank goodness Capricorn is only on the diurnal Ascendant for approximately one month!

Instead of feeling sorry for oneself, put the Capricorn energy into getting rid of old, useless items. There will be great affinity with dark areas such as attics and basements. The native should clean out these rooms and enjoy the surprise feeling of accomplishment and pride in having something in apple pie order. Those items should not be thrown away; instead, have a garage sale.

People from the past come into the native's life, as he or she runs into old friends or hears from relatives who have been out of touch for ages. There may be dealings with political people or rallies, the police department, a councilman, a mayor, a former boss. Now is not the time to make career changes, no matter how hard one believes he or she is working without being appreciated. This is a good time to visit parents, grandparents, or older members of the family.

What the native will be depressed about, and who is going to be a source of concern or require additional responsibility is indicated by the natal house position of Capricorn.

Check the condition of transiting and natal Saturn (ruler of Capricorn).

A visit to the dentist may be in order concerning fillings or dentures. Vitality is at its lowest peak and the native seems to lack energy for anything. If the blahs don't get him or her, aching knees will. One should keep warm and consume a lot of hot fluids such as tea and soup. Better days are coming.

Transiting or natal Saturn positioned in the diurnal first house will produce the same effect as Capricorn on the diurnal Ascendant.

Aquarius

Having survived a boring month, the native is now ready for excitement and the unconventional. The native doesn't have to look for it because it will find him or her. The unexpected generally occurs when Aquarius is on the diurnal Ascendant.

Activities are erratic, and the native is drawn into situations that vary from one day to the next. The element of the unexpected takes place either in the workplace, the home, or through relatives or friends. One may feel like rebelling against old, existing conditions, such as a desire to go into a new and unique field. Thinking twice before going off on a tangent is important as the native may regret it later after returning to the old self. Better alternatives are to purchase a CB, a harmless outlet offering a different way of meeting new people and making new friends, join a club or organization, or study astrology or attend an astrological meeting. Friends and their affairs may consume a good bit of the native's time. If natal or transiting Uranus is afflicted, one should avoid installing electrical wiring or purchasing electrical appliances.

What unexpected event may happen or who it will concern is indicated by the natal house position of Aquarius.

Check the condition of transiting and natal Uranus (ruler of Aquarius).

Unexpected injuries occur or there are problems with cramps in the lower limbs and calves.

Transiting or natal Uranus positioned in the diurnal first house will produce the same effect as Aquarius on the diurnal Ascendant.

Pisces

The native's nerves are shot from all the unexpected events last month, and it is time to seek seclusion, temporarily escaping from reality by indulging in a good book, listening to new music, going fishing, making a dress, or playing an instrument. Finding a constructive outlet for escapism is wise or one may take drugs or overindulge in alcoholic beverages.

The desire to work quietly or clandestinely will be strong, and others should be advised of the need for solitude and seclusion at this time. The native should not let others take advantage of him or her. Now is the time to enjoy feeling a bit lazy, as he or she will be busy enough when the diurnal Ascendant changes to Aries.

One can take up meditation at this time for it can bring peace of mind and soul. There may be an air of confusion, chaos, or secrecy about the native. If secret enemies have been working behind one's back, this is when they are most likely to be detected and brought out in the open.

Someone in the native's immediate circle may enter the hospital or become ill. It may be necessary to do some kind of undercover work or to be involved with the police. Someone may try to draw the native into a clandestine relationship. The native may drink too much or become involved with another individual who has overindulged in alcohol.

This is a period in which it is wise to remain behind the scenes and be as inconspicuous as possible. The native should not permit self-pity or inferiority complexes to bog him or her down.

Is someone going to the hospital? Why is there a need to escape at this time? Check the natal house position of Pisces.

Check the condition of transiting and natal Neptune (ruler of Pisces).

If the native has been having trouble with the feet, he or she should take time out for a rest period by elevating them on a cushion and turning on some soft music. Perhaps the shoes are not properly fitted; if so, purchase a new pair. Medication offered by anyone other than a physician should not be taken, and prescriptions should be checked to be sure they have not been confused with someone else's.

Transiting or natal Neptune positioned in the diurnal first house will produce the same effect as Pisces on the diurnal Ascendant.

Taking Tests
and Passing Exams

Not everyone will have the advantage of selecting the most opportune time for taking and passing tests, however it is possible in the case of written and driving tests for a drivers license or permit.

Such was the case of a young man who was attending summer school for drivers education. He was nervous about taking the written test and his mother asked me to select a suitable time and day for him. There wasn't too much time to do so as he needed his driver's permit within the following two weeks.

The first diurnal chart I erected had Cancer on the diurnal Ascendant, and I knew he would not be in a good emotional state because of that. So, I waited until his rising sign changed to Leo, offering more stability. The sign Leo also rules schools and, luckily, the Sun (ruler of Leo) was in Gemini, which rules short travels, driving, and oral and written tests and papers. All that was needed now was a good aspect from either a transiting or natal planet to his diurnal third house cusp to enhance third house matters of driving and test papers.

Chart #1 is his natal chart with only those transiting planets indicated that offered possibilities in helping him to pass the test.

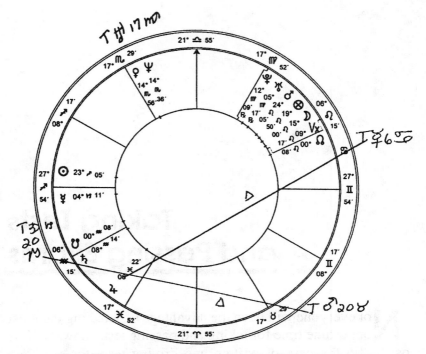

Chart #1, Natal Chart—December 15, 1962, 8:13 AM EST, Cleveland, Ohio, 81W41:44, 41N29:58

The transiting Moon was in the first house in Capricorn (Capricorn rules city government) and trining transiting Mars in the fifth house of schools and education. He also had transiting Mercury at six degrees Cancer trining his natal ruler, Jupiter, at six degrees Pisces. Uranus in his tenth house of government affairs did not make any close aspects to either natal or transiting planets.

Chart #2 is the diurnal chart for June 12, the day selected for his written exam. Leo is rising, giving him self-confidence and optimism. The ruling planet (Sun) is in Gemini, another positive sign and ruler of documents, papers, and written exams. His natal Jupiter in Pisces (ruler of police activity) is trining transiting Mercury in the twelfth house of police activity. Transiting Mercury rules his eleventh house of hopes and wishes and natal Jupiter rules the diurnal fifth house of schools. Transiting Moon is positioned in the sixth house (ruler of police and those of service

40

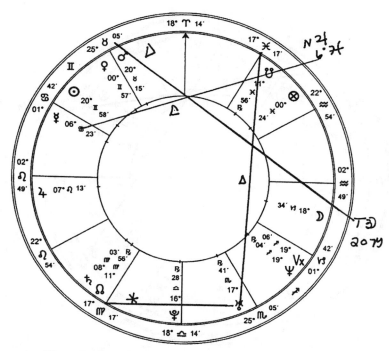

Chart #2, Diurnal Chart—June 12, 1979, 8:13 AM EST,
Cleveland, Ohio, 81W41:44, 41N29:58

to others) and in Capricorn (city government), trining transiting
Mars in the tenth house and ruling the tenth house of city
government.

The most important planet of all that assured this young man
success (he missed only one question on the exam) was transiting
Uranus. As noted, transiting Uranus was going through his tenth
house of city government. In the diurnal chart for June 12,
transiting Uranus is sextiling the third house cusp and trining the
ninth house cusp. Pisces rules jails and police buildings and Virgo
rules policemen and police activity.

Look closely and note that these two signs are positioned
natally on the third and ninth houses. Both third and ninth houses
are closely related to education and their affairs, including the
passing of tests, whether written or oral.

The diurnal chart helped determine the best *day* for taking a

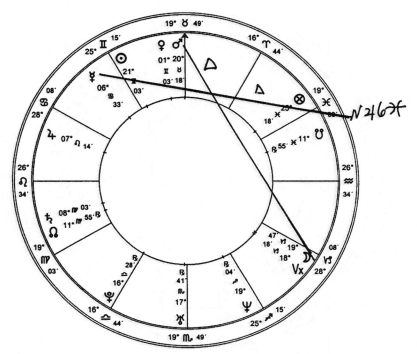

Chart #3,Event Chart—June 12, 1979, 11:15 AM EDT,
Parma, Ohio, 81W43:23, 41N24:17

drivers test. Now, an event chart was needed for the day to
determine the best *time*. Cleveland (Parma is a suburb), Ohio was
on Eastern Daylight Time on June 12, 1979, which meant it would
be four hours earlier than Universal Time (Greenwich Mean
Time), rather than five hours. Therefore, I suggested he take the
written exam as close to noon as possible. Chart #3 is the event
chart for June 12, 1979 at 11:15 a.m. Eastern Daylight Time.
Notice that transiting Mars is conjunct the tenth house cusp and
the transiting Moon in the event chart fifth house is trining both
transiting Mars and the event chart Midheaven. Transiting Mercury at 6 Cancer 33 in the eleventh house of hopes and wishes
(Mercury rules the eleventh house cusp) trines natal Jupiter at 6
Pisces in the seventh house and Jupiter rules the fifth house of
schools with transiting Moon therein throwing a favorable light
to transiting Mars in the tenth house. He passed with flying colors.

42

Winning at Lotteries,
Bingo, and the Races

Although four different charts were used in the winning of $15,000 through the Ohio lottery, it is not necessary to erect that many charts for bingo and the races, as can be seen in the various examples.

Chart #4 is a natal chart for the winner of the $15,000 lottery. There was a full Moon eclipse on May 25, 1975 at three degrees Sagittarius. Seven planets, both natal and transiting, were pulled into a trine and only two of these were affiliated in any way with money in the natal chart. The transiting Moon in the natal ninth house trined transiting Mars, ruler of the natal second house of money. Transiting Pluto, ruler of other people's money, received a sextile aspect from the eclipse position. The transiting Moon and Sun also sextiled and trined natal Jupiter and Uranus in the first house at three degrees Aries. Even though the conjunction to natal Saturn at two degrees Sagittarius was trine transiting Mars, ruler of the natal second house, it was felt that this restrictive energy of Saturn limited the winnings to $15,000, rather than one of the larger prizes.

Chart #5 is the diurnal chart calculated for the day of the full Moon eclipse. This chart offered a far different picture that held

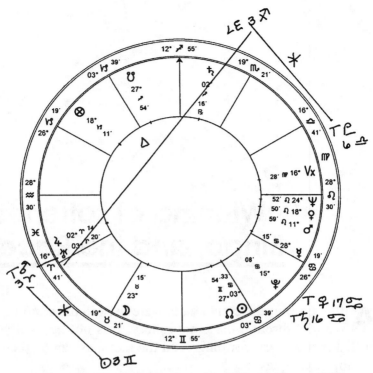

*Chart #4, Natal Chart—June 25, 1927, 11:00 p.m. EST,
Lakewood, Ohio, 81W48, 41N29*

more promise and actually induced the attempt to try for a
winning lottery ticket. The full Moon eclipse took place in the
diurnal tenth house of public recognition (one has to appear on
television in Ohio with a winning of $15,000 or more). The full
Moon trined three planets in the diurnal second house of money
and sextiled transiting Pluto, now in the diurnal eighth house of
other people's money. A second indication of not winning a larger
sum was transiting Saturn at sixteen degrees Cancer conjunct
transiting Venus at seventeen degrees Cancer (ruler of the natal
eighth house of other people's money).

A day would have to be selected on which the diurnal chart
would have natal or transiting Mars (ruler of the natal second
house of money) trining the natal tenth house (public recognition). This would be the diurnal chart's eleventh house. Six days

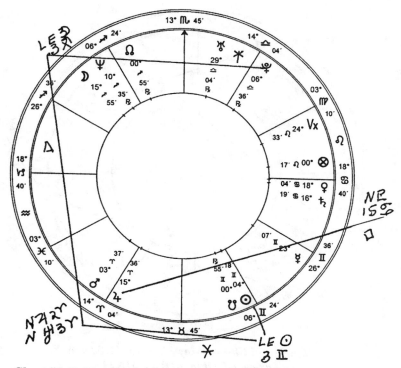

Chart #5, Eclipse Diurnal Chart—May 25, 1975, 11:00 p.m. EST,
Lakewood, Ohio, 81W48, 41N29

later on May 31, a diurnal chart was erected. Natal Mars at twelve degrees Leo was in an exact trine with the eleventh house cusp and sextiling the fifth house cusp of gambling. In Chart #6, the diurnal chart for May 31, note that transiting Uranus favorably trines the natal Ascendant at twenty-eight degrees Aquarius. This same planet, Uranus, is transiting through the native's natal eighth house.

Having the proper day selected, it is now time to select the most opportune time. Bear in mind that the diurnal chart remains the same for the entire day. The house cusps do not move. All that must be done is to determine what time of day the transiting Moon will conjunct either the second or eighth house cusp in the diurnal chart and purchase the raffle ticket or attend the bingo game at that time. Even a sextile or trine to the second or eighth house

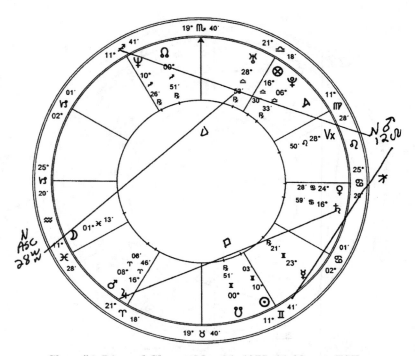

Chart #6, Diurnal Chart—May 31, 1975, 11:00 p.m. EST,
Lakewood, Ohio, 81W48, 41N29

cusp from the transiting Moon would be of great benefit.

Unfortunately, the transiting Moon would not cooperate on May 31. The transiting Moon was in a high degree of Aquarius and, with twelve degrees Pisces-Virgo on the second and eighth house cusps, there could not possibly be a conjunction or even a favorable aspect to the diurnal second or eighth house cusps.

In this case an event chart was erected for the time that Aquarius would be either on the second or eighth house cusp. The time selected was 10:07 a.m. Eastern Daylight Savings Time. Three degrees Leo is rising and natal Jupiter, Uranus, and Saturn all form a grand trine to the event chart's Ascendant sign. Best of all, this time was set when the transiting Moon was at twenty-four degrees Aquarius, exactly conjunct the eighth house cusp in the event chart. A lottery ticket was purchased at 10:07 a.m. on May 31, 1975, and won $15,000.

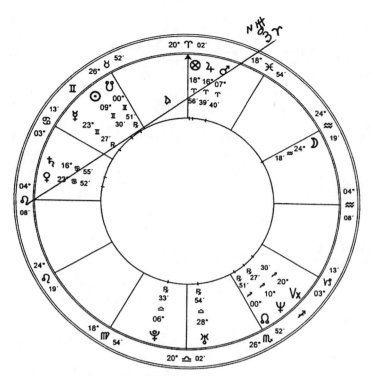

Chart #7, Event Chart—May 31, 1975, 10:07 a.m. EDT,
Cleveland, Ohio, 81W41:44, 41N29:58

If the ruler of the diurnal or natal second or eighth house cusp is trining the diurnal Ascendant, and the transiting Moon is in the same sign as the second or eighth house cusp, an event chart is not needed. All that is required is to determine what time the transiting Moon will be in the same degree that is positioned on the diurnal second or eighth house cusp and then purchase a lottery or raffle ticket at that time.

A Winning Bingo Chart

Chart #8 is a diurnal chart erected for January 12, 1979, the date the woman won $350 at a church bingo game. The transiting Moon is a timing device for the most favorable time to win, and with the conviction to quit when ahead, one can come out the winner.

To keep the diurnal chart clear and easy to read, Uranus and the transiting Moon are the only two planets illustrated. The woman has twenty degrees Cancer on the diurnal Ascendant. Her natal chart has two degrees Cancer rising.

Except for the difference in degrees, her natal and diurnal charts are quite similar. Uranus is transiting through both the natal and diurnal fifth house and making no apparent aspect to any of her natal or transiting planets on January 12.

One of the best and most favorable days for winning at bingo or the races, or purchasing raffle tickets is when a natal or transiting planet is trining the diurnal Ascendant. In this case, the native has twenty degrees Cancer on her diurnal Ascendant and transiting Uranus trines it form the fifth house of gambling, indicating a possibility of winning at games of chance and through other people's money (Uranus in Scorpio). Transiting Uranus is also the ruler of the diurnal eighth house.

Luckily, on this day the transiting Moon was in Cancer con-

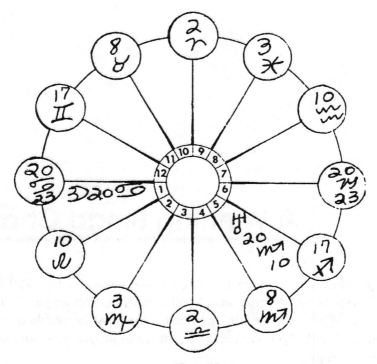

Chart #8
Diurnal Chart for January 12, 1979

junct the diurnal Ascendant and trining transiting Uranus in the diurnal fifth house. According to *Raphael's Ephemeris*, the transiting Moon would trine transiting Uranus on January 13 at 2:32 a.m. GMT. This aspect would occur approximately five hours earlier in Cleveland, Ohio (EST), making it 9:32 p.m. on January 12.

The transiting Moon is within orb of a degree for approximately two hours. She was told the most opportune time would be between 8:30 p.m. and 10:30 p.m. on January 12. She quit playing bingo shortly after 10:30 p.m., not because she was advised to do so, but because she was uncomfortable with the angry glares from other patrons (she had won every game except two—a feat one would not have believed possible).

The majority of my clients and students are winning at races and bingo games, and through the purchase of lottery tickets that pay off. I am not promising that you will win large amounts because you would have to have that potential in the natal chart. However, you will not be throwing your money away on useless lottery tickets as most of them will pay off in sums of $5 to $20, if not more.

Natal Chart Potentials

What are the potentials in the natal chart?

- Having transiting Jupiter in the natal second, fifth, eighth, or ninth house and conjunct the diurnal second or eighth house cusp, or trining the Ascendant.
- Having transiting Jupiter favorably aspecting the rulers of the natal second or eighth house and positioned in the diurnal second or eighth house.
- Having transiting Jupiter conjunct natal Uranus, Pluto, Jupiter, Sun or Moon. Purchase tickets or play the races at the time the transiting Moon conjuncts either the second or eight house cusp of an event chart or, if possible, the diurnal second or eighth house.

Winning

Follow these rules for winning at any time. This can occur more than twenty times a month.

- A lucky day is when a transiting or natal planet trines the diurnal Ascendant from the fifth or ninth house. Remember, an exact orb is required, or within a few minutes of exactitude.
- For even better luck, pick a day when the transiting or natal planet trining the diurnal Ascendant also rules either the natal or diurnal second or eighth house cusp.
- Another excellent day for winning large sums is when the natal or transiting ruler of the natal or diurnal second or eighth house cusp also has the opportunity to conjunct either the second or eighth house cusp in the diurnal chart. For example, a client with Sagittarius on his natal eighth house won $30,000 when natal Jupiter at twenty-one degrees Capricorn was conjunct the diurnal eighth house cusp at twenty-one degrees Capricorn. Luckily, the transiting Moon was in Tau-

rus and the time for purchasing the winning ticket was set for the time when the transiting Moon would reach twenty-one degrees Taurus and exactly trine both natal Jupiter and the diurnal eighth house cusp at twenty-one degrees Capricorn.

Generally speaking, any planet trining the diurnal Ascendant shows great potential for that particular day. It is for this reason that an exact orb is needed. By pushing the affairs indicated by the planet in trine aspect to the diurnal Ascendant, a project can be successfully pursued by the native.

If by chance a certain hour is needed for this successful enterprise (bingo, races, lottery ticket purchases), this is where the transiting Moon comes in. If lucky enough to have the transiting Moon trine that planet as indicated in the aspectarian section of *Raphael's Ephemeris*, then the time need only be subtracted for the particular locality. Otherwise, the time must be calculated when the Moon will reach that particular degree and conjunct or favorably aspect the second or eighth house cusp of the diurnal chart. Conjunctions of the Moon to the second or eighth house cusp are preferred for they seem to hold greater potential for success.

Proofreading
Lunations

Diurnal charts are the essence of proofreading what one sees in the natal chart at the time of new, full, or quarter Moons and eclipses.

Following a regular procedure in delineating diurnal charts erected for lunations may help one remain objective.

Orbs of Influence

All rules for lunations are amply covered in *Lunations and Predictions*, however the all-important orbs of influence will be repeated for convenience sake.

The allowable orb is ten degrees from new Moons, full Moons, quarter Moons, and eclipses to **transiting** planets.

The allowable orb is five degrees from new Moons, full Moons, and eclipses to **natal** planets.

Quarter Moons require a much closer orb of one degree to **natal** planets; otherwise, the impact does not seem to register.

The allowable orb is only one degree from **transiting** planets to **natal** planets on the day the diurnal chart is erected for a lunation.

The date, sign and degree of each new and full Moon are given

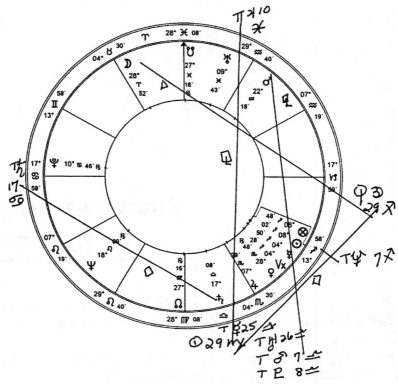

Chart #9, Natal Chart

at the top of each page in the *Rosicrucian Ephemeris*. The quarter Moon occurs approximately seven days after each new and full Moon and is illustrated by a square between the Sun and Moon in the aspectarian section.

The date, sign, and degree of each new and full Moon are given on the top of each page in *Raphael's Ephemeris*, while the quarter Moons are given at the bottom of each page.

For simplicity sake in reading the charts included here as examples, all minutes on the majority of planets have been rounded off to the nearest degree.

Procedure for Delineation

1. Chart #9 is a natal chart with the quarter Moon of September 23, 1974 on the outside and all the transiting planets for that day

exactly as they appear in the ephemeris.

2. The quarter Moon is positioned in this native's sixth house of work and health. It will be a week of great importance (quarter Moons operate within one week). The only aspect the quarter Moon makes to a natal planet is a trine to her natal Moon at twenty-eight degrees Aries. However, the transiting Sun at twenty-nine degrees Virgo inconjuncts her natal Moon.

3. The house and sign placement of the quarter Moon give an indication of what kind of activity may take place and who may be involved. The sixth house governs the second born child in a female's chart. The Moon at twenty-nine degrees Sagittarius is in a travel sign and in the third decanate, which has a Leo/Sun connotation. We have to assume that a child is planning to take a trip. This confirms that whatever takes place during the following week is likely to be centered around her second born child. When the ruler of the Moon's sign position in Sagittarius (Jupiter) is in hard aspect with the ruler of the Sun's sign position in Virgo (Mercury) and there are heavy aspects involving the ninth and the fifth houses, danger lies ahead for a child (the fifth house always indicates conditions surrounding a child, but the fourth and fifth houses generally determine which child. With the quarter Moon in the sixth house, we have to assume the events will concern her second born son.

4. It is of extreme importance to check the relationship between the ruler of the Moon's sign position and the ruler of the Sun's sign position. Transiting Jupiter is the ruler of the Moon's sign position in Sagittarius. Transiting Jupiter conjuncts her natal Uranus within one degree in her natal ninth house of distant matters. Transiting Mercury at twenty-five degrees Libra, ruler of the Sun's sign position in Virgo, is conjunct transiting Uranus at twenty-six degrees Libra, and both are sesquisquare natal Uranus and transiting Jupiter. We also have transiting Saturn conjunct her natal Ascendant and both are square her natal Saturn in her fourth house of family members. We have a loaded fourth house at the time of a quarter Moon with the addition of transiting Mars at seven degrees Libra conjunct transiting Pluto at eight

degrees Libra. Transiting Mars is the co-ruler of her natal tenth house and transiting Pluto is the ruler of her natal fifth house of children. Both transiting Mars and Pluto are sesquisquare her natal Mars at twenty-two degrees Aquarius in her natal eighth house of death. Notice that transiting Neptune at seven degrees Sagittarius conjuncts her natal Sun at eight degrees Sagittarius in her natal fifth house of children. If you count from the sixth house (her second born child), you will notice that transiting Saturn conjuncts the first house cusp, which is the eighth house of death of the second born child. Confirmations concerning a death in the family (fourth house stellium) are transiting Mercury and Uranus sesquisquare her natal Mars in her natal eighth house.

5. There are no less than five conjunctions and numerous hard aspects within the one degree allowable orb for transits at the time of a quarter Moon.

- Transiting Saturn conjunct natal Ascendant
- Transiting Jupiter conjunct natal Uranus
- Transiting Neptune conjunct natal Sun
- Transiting Mercury conjunct transiting Uranus
- Transiting Mars conjunct transiting Pluto
- Transiting Saturn square natal Saturn
- Transiting Mercury/Uranus conjucntion sesquisquare the natal Uranus/transiting Jupiter conjunction
- Transiting Mars/Pluto conjunction sesquisquare natal Mars

As you can see, there were far too many hard aspects that may indicate a disaster during the week ahead.

What happened? Her second born child (a nineteen year old son) celebrated his buddy's enlistment in the Marines with an all-night party. His buddy insisted on driving to Paris Island, South Carolina the next morning. His buddy fell asleep at the wheel of the car (Neptune rules the coma state of sleep) and crashed into a telephone pole. This woman's son went through the windshield and was killed instantly. My students can verify that I warned her not to let her son travel during the month of September. Unfortunately, after she left for work her son left a note telling her that he was driving his buddy to boot camp. The

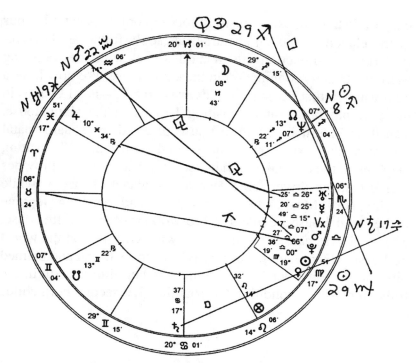

Chart #10, Diurnal Chart for Quarter Moon,
September 23, 1994

steering wheel protected his buddy, who survived the accident, suffering a broken arm, leg, and ribs.

6. A diurnal chart erected for the quarter Moon can serve as a proofreader for the events that were indicated in the natal chart. Chart #10 is the diurnal chart for September 23, 1974. The computer always adjusts the Moon and Sun according to the individual's time of birth. This woman was born during the evening hours. The quarter Moon occurred approximately eighteen hours earlier. The sign Taurus, at six degrees, is on the diurnal Ascendant. Transiting Mars and Pluto at six and seven degrees Libra inconjunct the diurnal Ascendant from the sixth house (her second born child) and also sesquisquare natal Mars in the eleventh house of friends. The significance of who was driving to boot camp lies with the eleventh house configurations. Transiting Jupiter at ten degrees Pisces rules the diurnal ninth house

cusp of distant states. Transiting Jupiter conjuncts natal Uranus in the eleventh house, indicating her son's friend as the Jupiter/Uranus conjunction are in hard aspect with the transiting Mercury/Uranus conjunction in the sixth house. We now have a confirmation that her son's buddy was driving—natal Uranus in the eleventh house and transiting Uranus in the sixth house. Tansiting Saturn in the third house of accidents squares natal Saturn in the sixth house (the second born child). Transiting Neptune in the diurnal eighth house conjunct natal Sun provides a clue that the driver fell asleep at the wheel of the car while driving. Natal Mars in the eleventh house and transiting Neptune in the eighth house are rulers and co-workers of the twelfth house. The death was caused by his buddy who fell asleep at the wheel of the car. His mother never forgave her son's friend and blamed him for her son's death. The stellium in her diurnal sixth house truly emphasized conditions surrounding her second born child.

Catalyst for
Slow Transits

The natal position of the diurnal Ascendant sign indicates the general trend for the month ahead. Chart #12 has Scorpio on the diurnal Ascendant and this sign is natally positioned on the sixth house of health (Chart #11).

Transiting Neptune is positioned in the diurnal first house. This young lady had to temporarily forego all gymnastic activities due to a health problem with her feet (Neptune rules the feet).

For further occurrences in the affairs of this young woman, look at transiting Pluto, ruler of the diurnal Ascendant. Transiting Pluto is positioned in her tenth house of public recognition (natally, her fifth house of schools and sports). She was to come before the public because of her athletic ability.

On February 8, 1979, transiting Sun and Mercury at nineteen degrees Aquarius trined the diurnal ruler, Pluto, from the third house of communication. The transiting Sun rules the ninth house of publications and Mercury the tenth house of honors and public recognition. Positioned in the sign Aquarius, it was an unexpected event.

Much to her parents' surprise, her picture appeared in the local paper, presenting her in beautiful form as she demonstrated her

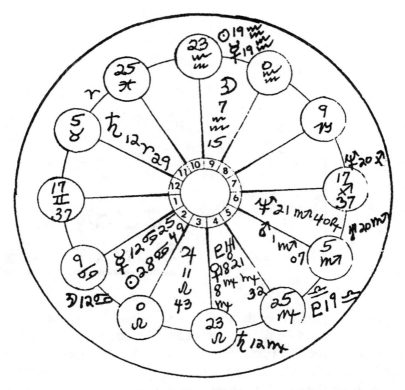

Chart #11
Natal Chart—Transits in outer circle

technique on the bars. She was participating in the state gymnastic championship just about the time she developed the health problem with her feet.

Another aspect responsible for bringing her before the public was transiting Saturn conjunct the diurnal tenth house cusp and sextiling natal Mercury at twelve degrees Cancer. The sextile between transiting Saturn and natal Mercury was a slow moving aspect that had been in effect for the previous fifteen days. It took a conjunction with an angular house cusp to serve as a catalyst for action.

Her parents discovered the picture in the newspaper at 11:00 a.m., just as the transiting Moon was conjunct natal Mercury at twelve degrees Cancer and sextiling both transiting Saturn and

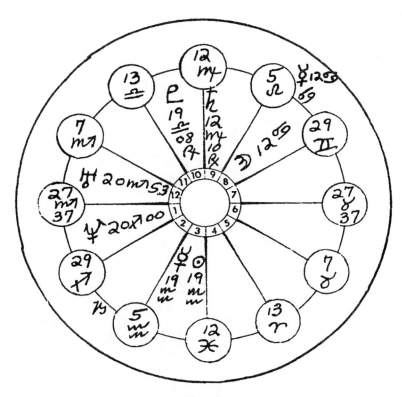

Chart #12
Diurnal Chart, February 8, 1979—Natal planet in outer circle

the tenth house cusp. Natal Mercury (ruler of her natal chart) and Pluto (ruler of the diurnal chart) were pleasantly aspected, making it an enjoyable and eventful day for her.

The fact she was unaware of her picture being taken for publication in the newspaper is indicated by transiting Uranus positioned in the twelfth house of secrets and ruling the third house of communication and news.

One final point to remember: A diurnal chart is erected for the time of birth. If the native was born around 7:00 p.m. and a certain event is indicated in the diurnal chart, it may not come to attention until the following day. The diurnal chart is in operation for a 24-hour period. Those who are born early in the morning generally feel the effects on the same day.

General Forecasting

Natal Moon Trine
Diurnal Ascendant

Libra is rising on the diurnal Ascendant and natally is positioned on the cusp of the seventh house.

This individual had a strong desire to socialize with others. On the day the natal Moon at nineteen degrees Aquarius was exactly trine her diurnal Ascendant at nineteen degrees Libra, she went out to dinner (Libra) with her female friends (Moon/women and Aquarius/friends). The trine promised her an enjoyable evening.

The transiting Moon in the diurnal first house sextile transiting Saturn in the eleventh house of friends confirmed a social gathering with friends because Leo, on the diurnal eleventh house cusp, is natally on the fifth house cusp of entertainment.

Transiting Saturn Square
Fourth and Tenth House Cusps

This is the diurnal chart of a businesswoman who performed a service and was not paid for it.

Transiting Saturn at eleven degrees Virgo is squaring both the fourth and tenth house cusps. Sagittarius is natally on the second

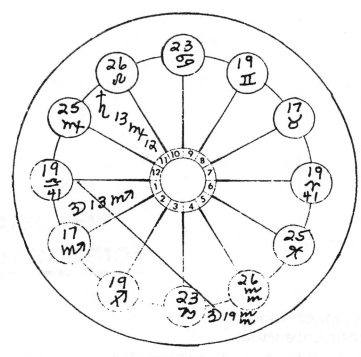

Chart #13

house cusp (personal finances), while Gemini is natally on the eighth house cusp (finances of others). Saturn is transiting through her natal tenth house of careers. Therefore, money would be related to work, but there would be trouble through it because of the square aspect.

Transiting Mercury, ruler of the diurnal Ascendant, is positioned in the diurnal sixth house of work and service to others. In Pisces, there could be possible deception through working conditions even though Mercury makes nor receives any adverse aspects at this time. Mercury was drawn into the situation because of its rulership of the diurnal Ascendant and the tenth house cusp which is being squared by transiting Saturn.

Saturn rules the diurnal fifth house cusp (children, youth, and young people), and transiting Venus is positioned in the diurnal fifth house. A young woman shrewdly took unfair advantage of the native and never paid her. Transiting Venus rules the diurnal

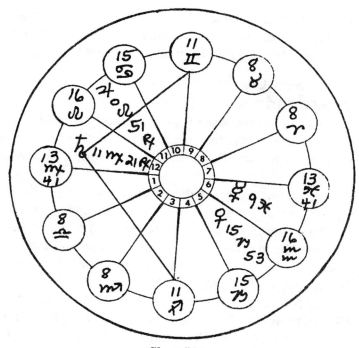

Chart #14

second house of money. One would think that Venus in Capricorn would age the woman, however, in the fifth house, she was a young woman of a serious nature. Jupiter, ruler of the fourth house cusp and being squared by Saturn, is in Leo, confirming the element of youth. It was later discovered she was a Capricorn (Venus in the fifth house in Capricorn).

Whenever a transiting planet squares a house cusp, look to the house the planet rules in the diurnal chart. If there are no planets therein to give a basic clue as to who is involved with the square, then look to its natural house rulership. In this case, Saturn rules the diurnal fifth house as Capricorn is on the house cusp and also would have some effect on the tenth house of careers, being its natural ruler.

There were no planets in the tenth house, but Venus in the fifth house offered the basic clue. If neither of these houses had planets positioned in them, then look to the rulers of the houses being squared and try to determine the course of action from them. In this case, look to both transiting Mercury, ruler of the diurnal tenth house, and transiting Jupiter, ruler of the diurnal fourth house.

Transiting Mercury Trine Diurnal Ascendant

Libra is on the diurnal Ascendant and natally is positioned on the eighth house cusp. Matters pertaining to death, sex, or money belonging to others will come to the fore during the ensuing month.

Transiting Venus, ruler of the diurnal Ascendant, is in the diurnal third house of communication, documents, newspapers, and news. Sagittarius on the cusp of the third house is natally positioned on the native's tenth house of careers and public recognition. This brings news and communication to do with one's public image or career.

Transiting Mercury at twenty-two degrees Aquarius, natural ruler of the third house of communication and news, is trining the diurnal Ascendant at twenty-two degrees Libra. Mercury rules the diurnal eleventh house of friends and the ninth house of publications.

A friend (Mercury in Aquarius ruling the diurnal eleventh house) wrote a complimentary newspaper article (Mercury rules the ninth house of publications) concerning the native's career in dealing with murder and rape cases (Libra on the diurnal Ascendant and natally positioned on the eighth house of death and sex). In the natal chart, Mercury in Aquarius is transiting through the native's natal twelfth house, indicating that the article was written secretly without her knowledge. Venus in Capricorn, ruler of the diurnal Ascendant, is transiting the native's natal eleventh house of friends (an old woman friend submitted the article).

A few weeks later, when transiting Venus, ruler of the diurnal Ascendant, reached twelve degrees Capricorn and trined transiting Saturn in the diurnal eleventh house of friends, the native received a phone call (Venus still in the diurnal third house) from an old friend (Venus in Capricorn and Saturn in the eleventh

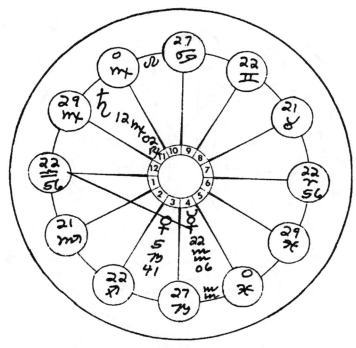

Chart #15

house are indicative of old friends or those from the past). The native had not seen or heard from this friend in a long time and the surprising news was that the friend is now an insurance agent (Libra on the diurnal Ascendant, positioned on the native's eighth house, governing insurance).

Transiting Moon Square Diurnal Ascendant

This is a simple chart to read as only the transiting Moon and Sun are illustrated. On January 5, 1979, the quarter Moon was positioned at fourteen degrees Aries and the Sun at fourteen degrees Capricorn. The quarter Moon position made no aspect whatever to any natal planets.

However, the transiting Moon is the ruler of the diurnal Ascendant and also squares the diurnal Ascendant. At the same time, the Sun at fourteen degrees Capricorn is opposing the diurnal

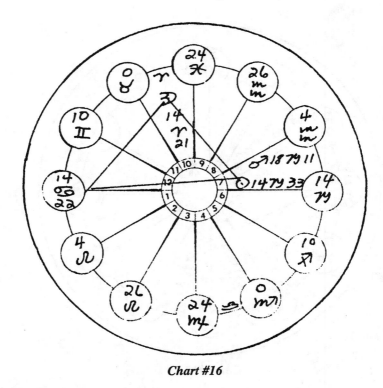

Chart #16

Ascendant.

What happened? She was late getting to work (transiting Moon in the diurnal tenth house) due to mechanical problems (Moon in Aries) with her car (Sun in Capricorn rules the diurnal third house of travel). The transiting Sun's position in Capricorn also governs delays and she was three hours late for work.

A Trine and A Square to Diurnal Ascendant

Leo is rising on the diurnal Ascendant and natally is positioned on the fifth house cusp governing conditions to do with children, romance, and gambling.

The natal Sun at twenty-one degrees Aries is trining the diurnal Ascendant at twenty-one degrees Leo, ruler of the diurnal Ascendant. This man attended a bingo game and won two prizes amounting to $50.

This would have been a far luckier aspect had his natal Moon at twenty-one degrees Scorpio (other people's money) not squared his diurnal Ascendant at the same time. And, the transiting Moon offered no assistance either.

Sports Gaming
Can Be Loads of Fun

I don't profess to have all the answers to the selection of which team will win the game, but this system has proven itself in accuracy far better than other systems I have experimented with over the past twenty years. With three planets natally in Leo, it is not surprising that I would be interested in sports gaming. The rules for using diurnal charts with sports gaming are far different from those used with diurnal charts for individuals. The following rules can apply to baseball, basketball, football, and hockey games.

- A natal chart for each team is officially used on the day, time, and place that each team plays its *first official* game of the season. You only have to set up one natal chart for each team; the planets therein will be supplied to the angular house cusps of the diurnal chart.
- Use a diurnal chart for each game following the opening game. Use the exact time and place that was used to set up the natal chart. The only difference will be the date for each game played.
- The diurnal or natal planetary aspects to angular house cusps in the diurnal charts are the only configurations used with my

system of sports gaming.

- Only one degree of orb is permitted from natal and diurnal planets to angular house cusps in the diurnal chart. However, an exact aspect is preferable.

- Aspects between transiting planets are never used as you will notice they are often similar in both competitive diurnal charts.

- However, aspects between diurnal or natal planets are very important if they both aspect an angular house cusp simultaneously in the diurnal chart.

- The Part of Fortune often aids in determining a winner. If the diurnal or natal Part of Fortune squares, semisquares, or sesquisquares an angular house cusp, this team may lose the game.

- However, if one team has a soft aspect to an angular house cusp from the diurnal or natal Part of Fortune and the other team has a soft aspect to an angular house cusp from the diurnal or natal Vertex, the team with the Vertex will win over the Part of Fortune. I don't know why but a sextile or trine to the tenth house cusp from the Vertex appears to have more strength than the Part of Fortune (the only aspect that the diurnal Vertex can make to an angular house cusp is a sextile or trine to the diurnal tenth house cusp or an opposition to the diurnal Ascendant). Unfortunately, I cannot provide any insight with the Vertex in opposition with the diurnal Ascendant as I have never had a game chart with this kind of configuration.

- Give first consideration to squares, semisquares, sesquisquares, oppositions, and inconjuncts. They are the most important aspects in sports gaming, especially with winners.

- Sextiles and trines from the diurnal or natal planets to the angles of the diurnal chart don't seem to assist very much with winners. However, there is an exception to this rule. The diurnal or natal Part of Fortune or the diurnal or natal Vertex can be one of the deciding factors.

- The team with the most aspects to angular house cusps from diurnal or natal planets has the greatest potential for winning, **especially** if the team has a sort of modified T-square formation to an angular house cusp. This aspect will be fully illustrated and called to your attention in the following diurnal charts.

Cleveland vs. Houston, June 30, 1997

Notice that all the configurations for setting up the diurnal chart are exactly the same as the natal chart with the exception of the date for which this game was played.

On June 30, 1997, the Cleveland Indians beat the Houston Astros.

Set your eyes on the modified T-square to the first house cusp of the diurnal chart for the Cleveland Indians, as well as these configurations:

- The diurnal Moon at twenty-five degrees Taurus sesquis-quares the diurnal Ascendant.

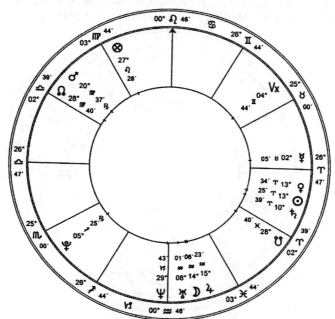

Chart #17, Natal Chart, Cleveland Indians—April 2, 1997, 7:35 p.m. PST, Oakland, California, 122W16:11, 37N48:16

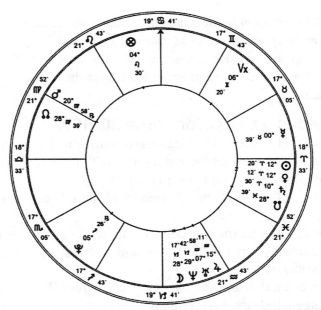

*Chart #18, Natal Chart, Houston Astros—April 1, 1997, 7:05
p.m. CST, Houston, Texas, 95W21:47, 29N45:47*

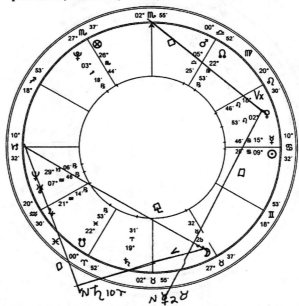

*Chart #19, Diurnal Chart, Cleveland Indians—June 30, 1997,
7:35 p.m. PST, Oakland, California, 122W16:11, 37N48:16*

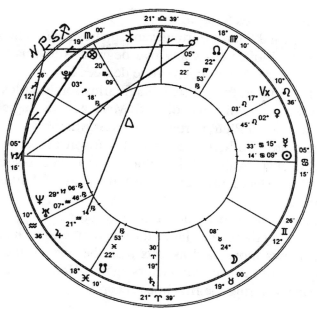

*Chart #20, Diurnal Chart, Houston Astros—June 30, 1997,
7:05 p.m. CST, Houston, Texas, 95W21:47, 29N45:47*

- Natal Saturn at ten degrees Aries squares the first house cusp.
- The diurnal Moon at twenty-five degrees Taurus semisquares natal Saturn at ten degrees Aries, creating what I have termed a modified T-square.
- The diurnal Venus at two degrees Leo squares the diurnal tenth house cusp.
- The diurnal Venus at two degrees Leo squares natal Mercury at two degrees Taurus, which conjuncts the diurnal fourth house cusp.
- There are two hard aspects to the first house cusp, including a modified T-square.
- There are two aspects to the tenth house cusp: one square from diurnal Venus and one opposiiton from natal Mercury.

The diurnal chart for the Houston Astros for June 30, 1997 shows these configurations:

- Diurnal Mars at five degrees Libra squares the first house cusp at five degrees Capricorn.
- Diurnal Mars semisquares the diurnal Part of Fortune at

twenty degrees Scorpio.

- The diurnal Part of Fortune semisquares the first house cusp.
- Diurnal Jupiter at twenty-one degrees Aquarius trines the tenth house cusp at twenty-one degrees Libra.
- Natal Pluto at five degrees Sagittarius semisextiles the first house cusp while the diurnal Mars at five degrees Libra sextiles natal Pluto at five degrees Sagittarius.
- There are two hard aspects and one soft aspect to the first house cusp. Although it includes a modified T-square, it is not considered favorable when the Part of Fortune is involved.
- There is one trine to the tenth house cusp.

In weighing these two charts, the one for the Cleveland Indians clearly shows more hard aspects than the one for the Houston Astros. One of the deciding factors against Houston was the Part of Fortune squaring the first house cusp.

Cleveland Vs. Houston, July 1, 1997

On July 1, 1997, the Cleveland Indians beat the Houston Astros.

The diurnal chart for the Cleveland Indians shows:

- One of the most significant aspects is an opposition from the seventh house to the first house. The diurnal Sun, within a one degree orb, opposes the first house cusp.
- Natal Saturn at ten degrees Aries squares the first house cusp within the one degree allowable orb.
- There is a genuine T-square aspect with the diurnal Sun and the first house cusp, both in square apsect with natal Saturn.
- Diurnal Venus is still within orb of squaring the tenth house cusp.
- There are two hard aspects to the first house cusp, which in turn create a real T-square.
- There is one hard aspect to the tenth house cusp.

The diurnal chart for the Houston Astros shows:

- The diurnal Moon inconjuncts the first house cusp.
- The diurnal Moon sesquisquares the tenth house cusp.

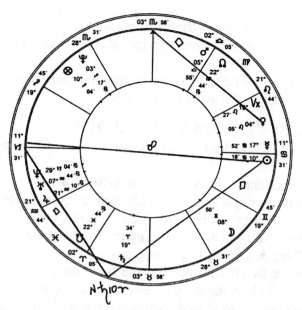

Chart #21, Diurnal Chart, Cleveland Indians—July 1, 1997, 7:35 p.m. PST, Oakland, California, 122W16:11, 37N48:16

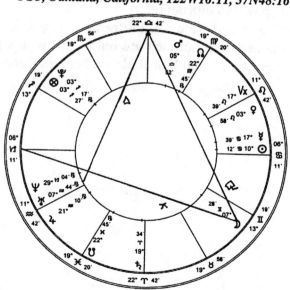

Chart #22, Diurnal Chart, Houston Astros—July 1, 1997, 7:05 p.m. CST, Houston, Texas, 95W21:47, 29N45:47

- Diurnal Jupiter trines the tenth house cusp.
- There were no T-squares or a modified version of one in this chart.
- There is only one hard aspect to the first house cusp and one hard aspect to the tenth house cusp.

Cleveland Vs. Houston, July 2, 1997

On July 2, 1997, the Houston Astros beat the Cleveland Indians.

The diurnal chart for the Houston Astros shows:
- Diurnal Mars at six degrees Libra squares the first house cusp.
- Diurnal Jupiter semisquares the first house cusp.
- Diurnal Mars exactly sesquisquares Jupiter, creating a modified T-square to the first house cusp.
- There are two hard aspects to the first house cusp.

The diurnal chart for the Cleveland Indians shows:
- There were no modified T-squares in this chart.
- The transiting Sun at eleven degrees Cancer opposes the first house cusp within one degree.
- The natal Sun and Venus at thirteen degrees Aries squares the first house cusp but they are out of orb with a possible square from the diurnal Sun at eleven degrees Cancer.

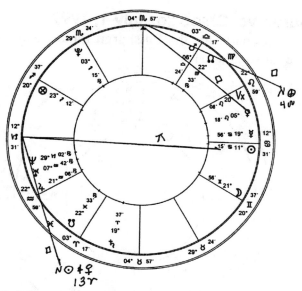

Chart #23, Diurnal Chart, Cleveland Indians—July 2, 1997, 7:35 p.m. PST, Oakland, California, 122W16:11, 37N48:16

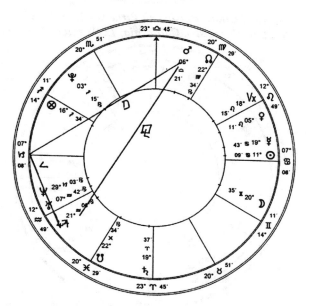

Chart #24, Diurnal Chart, Houston Astros—July 2, 1997, 7:05 p.m. CST, Houston, Texas, 95W21:47, 29N45:47

Pittsburgh vs. Chicago, July 1, 1997

The natal charts for the Pittsburgh Pirates and the Chicago Cubs are illustrated below.

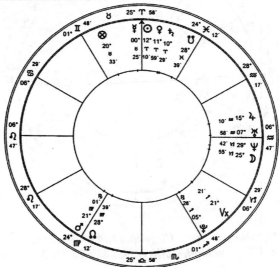

Chart #25, Natal Chart, Pittsburgh Pirates—April 1, 1997, 1:05 p.m.
PST, San Francisco, California, 122W25:06, 37N46:30

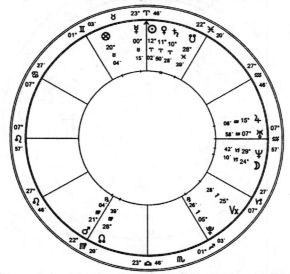

Chart #26, Natal Chart, Chicago Cubs—April 1, 1997,
1:05 p.m. EST, Toronto, Ontario, 79W23, 43N39

I don't have the score for this game between Pittsburgh and Chicago, but no doubt it was a close one as you will see from their diurnal charts. I usually pass up a game when there is a great deal of similarity between the two charts. Pittsburgh won the game.

- Pittsburgh had a modified T-square and a yod, all within the one degree orb of influence.
- Diurnal Jupiter at twenty-one degrees Aquarius inconjuncts the tenth house cusp at twenty degrees Cancer and natal Mars at twenty-one degrees Virgo.
- Natal Mars at twenty-one degrees Virgo sextiles the tenth house cusp, creating the yod formation in Pittsburgh's diurnal chart.
- The diurnal Vertex at twenty-one degrees Taurus sextiles the tenth house cusp, exactly trines natal Mars at twenty-one degrees Virgo, and squares diurnal Jupiter at twenty-one degrees Aquarius.
- Diurnal Jupiter squares the diurnal Vertex and inconjuncts the diurnal tenth house cusp, thus creating another important aspect configuration.
- The diurnal Vertex trines natal Mars and both throw a favorable aspect to the tenth house cusp.
- The diurnal Moon sesquisquaares the diurnal Ascendant within the one degree allowable orb.

As you can see, there were countless aspects to the diurnal tenth house cusp and one aspect to the diurnal first house cusp. Note that Pittsburgh's Vertex was highly activated.

Chicago's diurnal chart had a great deal of similiarity with Pittsburgh's diurnal chart. Both Pittsburgh and Chicago had the same yod formation involving diurnal Jupiter at twenty-one degrees Aquarius, the tenth house cusp, and natal Mars at twenty-one degrees Virgo; natal Mars sextiled the tenth house cusp, which created the yod formation.

There was one major difference between the two charts. Chicago did not have a Vertex aspect. Instead, it had the natal Part of Fortune square diurnal Jupiter at twenty-one degrees Aquarius and trine natal Mars at twenty-one degrees Virgo.

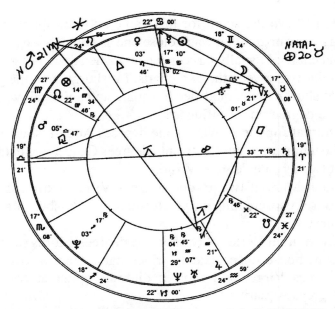

Chart #27, Diurnal Chart, Pittsburgh Pirates—July 1, 1997, 1:05 p.m.
PST, San Francisco, California, 122W25:06, 37N46:30

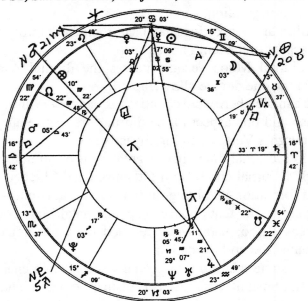

Chart #28, Diurnal Chart, Chicago Cubs, July 1, 1997,
1:05 p.m. EST, Toronto, Ontario, 79W23, 43N39

Other aspects in the chicago chart are:

- Both natal Part of Fortune and natal Mars sextile the tenth house cusp.
- Diurnal Mercury at seventeen degrees Cancer squares the diurnal first house cusp.

With such close similarity in aspects to angular house cusps, the deciding factor lies with Pittsburgh's diurnal Vertex over Chicago's Part of Fortune.

Texas vs. Los Angeles, July 1, 1997

The natal charts for Texas and Los Angeles are illustrated below and on the next page.

Texas beat Los Angeles on July 1, 1997.

The diurnal chart for Texas shows:

- An important aspect configuration was created with diurnal Jupiter at twenty-one degrees Aquarius trine the diurnal first house cusp and inconjunct natal Mars at twenty-one degrees Virgo, which, in turn, semisextiles the first house cusp.
- The natal Moon forms a conjunction with the fourth house cusp.

As you can see, there was very little activity with Texas's chart.

The Los Angeles diurnal chart has this configuration:

- The natal Part of Fortune at twenty-two degrees Taurus squares diurnal Jupiter at twenty-one degrees Aquarius and the Part of Fortune also inconjucnts the diurnal first house cusp.

That was the only aspect in Los Angeles's diurnal chart. No special aspect formation was created because diurnal Jupiter at twenty-one degrees Aquarius was two degrees away from a trine to the first house cusp at twenty-three degrees Libra.

The Texas diurnal chart had an aspect configuration plus natal Moon in opposition to the tenth house cusp.

In closing, you will have to work with numerous natal and diurnal charts to get a clear picture of which team has greater strength over the other in its diurnal chart.

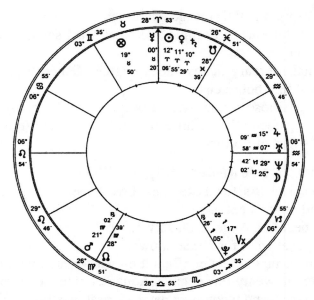

Chart #29, Natal Chart, Texas, April 1, 1997,
1:35 p.m. CST, Arlington, Texas, 97W06, 32N44

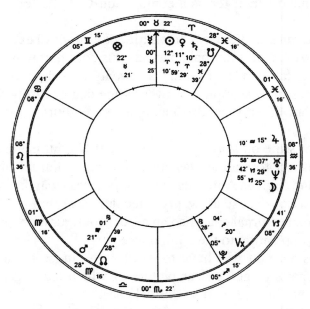

Chart #30, Natal Chart, Los Angeles—April 1, 1997,
1:05 p.m. PST, Los Angeles, California, 118W14:34, 34N03:08

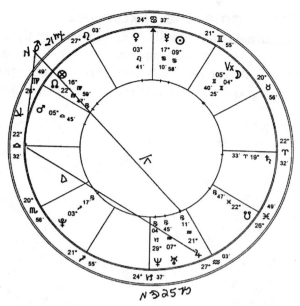

Chart #31, Diurnal Chart, Texas—July 1, 1997
1:35 p.m. CST, Arlington, Texas, 97W06, 32N44

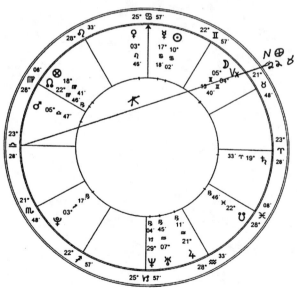

Chart #32, Diurnal Chart, Los Angeles—July 1, 1997,
1:05 p.m. PST, Los Angeles, California, 118W14:34, 34N08:08

Three More Game Chart Examples

Only the diurnal charts are illustrated for each of the six teams. All three games were played on July 4, 1997. I was busy with Fourth of July festivities and only selected these three games. The scores are inlcuded along with all the aspect configurations drawn in them.

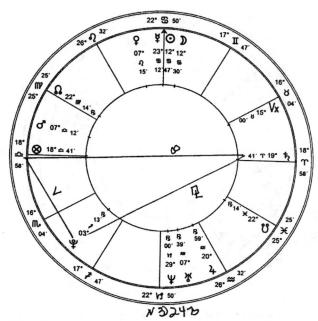

I picked Toronto, the underdog. Toronto beat New York, 1-0.

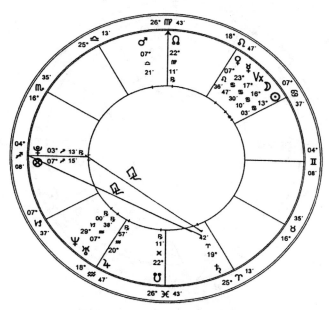

New York lost to Toronto, 1-0.

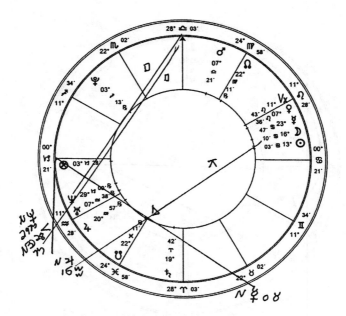

I picked Minnesota. Minnesota beat Milwaukee, 13-0.

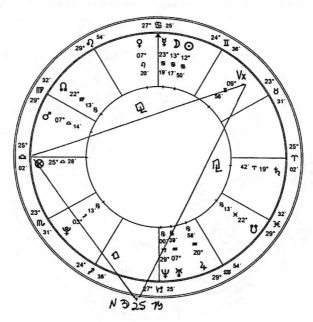

Milwaukee lost to Minnesota, 13-0.

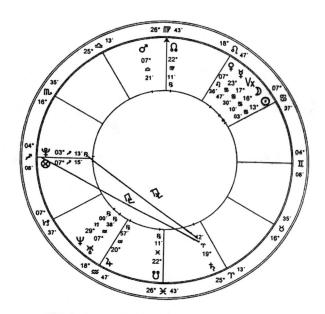

I picked Seattle. Seattle beat Anaheim, 8-4.

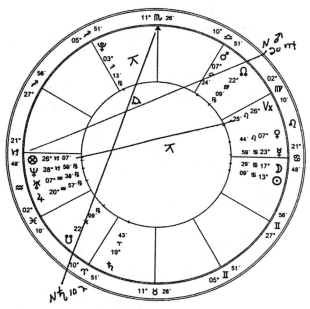

Anaheim lost to Seattle, 8-4.

Another Method
for Sports Gaming

There is one major drawback with the use of diurnal charts!
Each pair of teams that played against each other during the
first game of the season will have the same natal chart. When they
play opposite each other again during the baseball season, they
will also have the same diurnal chart. There is no way you will
be able to determine the winner when this happens.

Your only alternative is to forget about using diurnal charts and
instead use one chart that has been set up for the time and place
for the home team. In fact, you may even prefer this method of
picking winners because you only have one chart to work with.
The previous system of using diurnal charts applies the use of the
natal and the diurnal charts together.

This second method for determining winners of baseball, basketball, football, and hockey games uses an event chart which is,
as stated above, set up for the time and location where the home
team is playing.

Rules

- Keep a close orb of not more than two degrees between the
  transiting planets. Two degrees and thirty minutes is okay but

I would not use three degrees. Use a closer orb for aspects from planets to the angular house cusps, preferably exact, but one degree orb is fine.

- Every newspaper provides you with the time and place for each game that will be played the following day. Be careful, because your local newspaper may be using the time that the game will be televised in your local area. If, for example, you live in Chicago and the Chicago White Sox are playing in Los Angeles, your newspaper may list the game as 9:05 p.m. CDT. However, the game is being played in Los Angeles so the actual starting time would be 7:05 p.m. CDT. The 7:05 p.m. PDT time is the correct time to use for this game along with the latitude and longitude for Los Angeles. Always keep these time changes for various zones in mind when setting up a chart for any game being played in the city of the home team.

I don't have the slightest idea what others use for determining winners for sporting games. However, I have tremendous success with the following method. The easiest way to do this is to write down all the aspects on a piece of paper, taking great care to group together those that are activating angular houses or their rulers.

- I use houses one through six for the home team with an emphasis placed on the *first and fourth houses* and rulers thereof.
- I use houses seven through twelve for the visitor's team with an emphasis on the *seventh and tenth houses* and rulers thereof.
- If the home team has more aspects involving the first and/or the fourth houses, the home team wins.
- If the visitor's team has more aspects involving the seventh and tenth houses, the visitor's team wins.
- You should have one or both of the following configurations to determine the winning team: 1) Look for lots of aspects to planets in angular houses and 2) look for lots of aspects involving the ruler of an angular house cusp.
- If you come up with a large groups of aspects with seventh

or tenth house configurations, the visiting team is likely to win.

- If you come up with a large group of aspects with first or fourth house configurations the home team will win.
- It doesn't seem to matter whether the aspects are hard of soft. What does matter is how much activity and energy is being generated towards an angular house or the rulers.

Home Team Wins, 5-1

There is heavy emphasis on the *fourth house*, which belongs to the home team. They won with a score of 5-1.

- Jupiter is in the third house and conjuncts the *fourth house* cusp.
- The Moon is in the eleventh house and sesquisquares Jupiter, which in turn conjuncts the *fourth house* cusp.

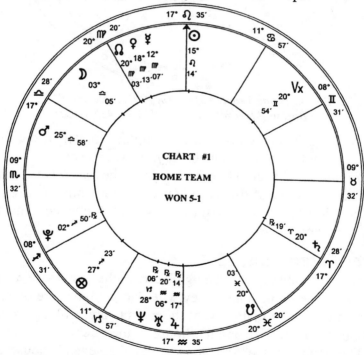

Pittsburgh Home Team, August 7, 1997, 1:35 p.m. EDT, Pittsburgh, Pennsylvania, 79W59:46, 40N26:26

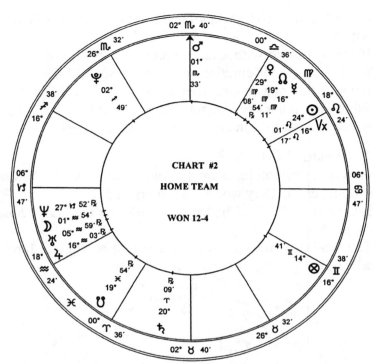

Boston Home Team, August 16, 1997, 5:05 p.m. EDT,
Boston, Massachusetts, 71W03:37, 42N21:30

- Venus is in the tenth house inconjunct Jupiter in the third house and Jupiter conjuncts the *fourth house cusp*.
- Venus is in the tenth house inconjunct the *fourth house cusp*.
- The Sun, ruler of the tenth house, is in the ninth house and inconjunct Jupiter in the third house with Jupiter conjunct the *fourth house cusp*.

Home Team Wins, 12-4

There is great emphasis being placed on the first house, which belongs to the home team. They won with a high score of 12-4. It doesn't seem to matter what the aspects are, as long as they continue to activate an angular house or the rulers.

- The Moon in the *first house* rules the seventh house and squares Mars in the ninth house (which is bad for the visitor's team because the Moon is the ruler of their seventh house cusp).

- The Moon in the *first house* sesquisquares Mercury in the eighth house.
- The Moon in the *first house* squares the tenth house cusp (the visitor's tenth).
- The Moon in the *first house* sextiles Pluto in the eleventh house with Pluto ruling the tenth.
- Uranus is in the *first house* inconjunct the seventh house cusp.
- Venus, ruler of the fourth house cusp, is in the eighth house and trines Neptune in the *first house*.

Note: The Moon is the ruler of the seventh house cusp and squares the tenth house cusp. Yes, the Moon also squares the fourth house cusp. However, the Moon, being the ruler of the seventh house, will feel the hard aspect to the tenth with greater emphasis because the tenth and the seventh houses belong to the visitor's team.

Visiting Team Wins, 10-5

- The Moon, ruler of the *seventh house*, is in the eighth house trine Jupiter in the first house; Jupiter rules the eleventh house. The eighth, seventh, and eleventh houses are emphasized; they belong to the visitor's team.
- The Moon, ruler of the *seventh house*, in the eighth house, semisquares Pluto in the *tenth house*; Pluto rules the *tenth house*.
- The Sun, co-ruler of the *seventh house* and positioned in the *seventh house*, opposes Jupiter in the first house with Jupiter ruling the eleventh house of the visitor's side of the chart.

An emphasis on the *seventh and tenth houses*, a planet in the seventh house (Sun), and the ruler of the seventh house (Moon) are all highlighted.

Other factors to consider:

- Venus, ruler of the *fourth house*, in the eighth house, inconjuncts Saturn in the second house and Saturn rules the *first house*. (Note that the ruler of the fourth house—Venus—inconjuncts the ruler of the first house—Saturn.) The rulers of

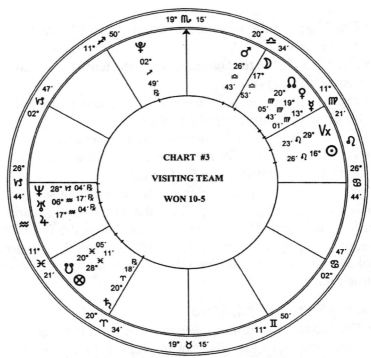

19° ♏ 15'

*Cincinnati Home Team, August 8, 1997, 7:35 p.m. EDT,
Cincinnati, Ohio, 84W27:25, 39N09:43*

the first and fourth houses are in hard aspect with one another.
The home team generally loses when this happens.

- If the ruler of the seventh house cusp make a hard aspect to
  the ruler of the tenth house cusp, or vise versa, and other
  aspects confirm, the visiting team generally loses.
- Never limit the aspects to houses only as illustrated in the first
  two charts for the home team.
- Always look for aspects to activate the ruler of the seventh or
  tenth house cusp with at least one planet in the seventh or
  tenth house also aspected for the visiting team to win.
- Always look for aspects to activate the ruler of the first or
  fourth house cusp with at least one planet in the first or fourth
  aspected at the same time for the home team to win.

96

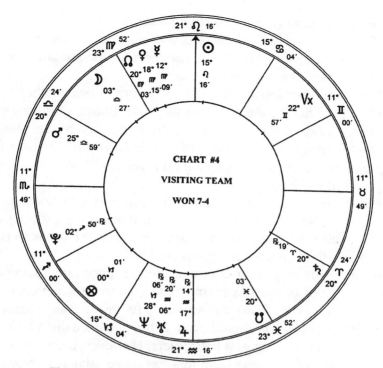

*Chicago Home Team, August 7, 1997, 1:20 p.m. CDT,
Chicago, Illinois, 87W39, 41N51*

Visiting Team Wins, 7-4

With the *tenth house* heavily highlighted and also the *seventh
house*, the visiting team won with a score of 7-4.

- Mercury, ruler of the eighth and eleventh houses, in the *tenth
  house* semisquares Mars in the twelfth house; Mars rules the
  home team's sixth house cusp.
- Mercury, ruler of the eighth and eleventh houses, in the *tenth
  house* sextiles the Ascendant and trines the *seventh house
  cusp*.
- Mercury, ruler of the eighth and eleventh houses, in the *tenth
  house* sesquisquares Neptune in the third; Neptune rules the
  fifth house cusp (Neptune in the third house and ruler of the
  fifth house pertains to the home team).
- Venus in the *tenth house* inconjuncts Jupiter in the third

house; Jupiter rules the second house.

- The Sun, ruler of the *tenth house cusp*, in the ninth house opposes Jupiter in the third; Jupiter rules the second house, which belongs to the home team.

There are other aspects that are within orb of one another:

- Saturn, ruler of the third, in the sixth house sesquisquare Pluto, ruler of the first house cusp, in the first house. (Note that Saturn is in the lower half of the chart which pertains to the home team and makes a hard aspect to Pluto in the first, ruler of the first.)
- Mars, ruler of the sixth house, is in the twelfth house and squares Neptune in the third house, ruler of the fifth house (the third, fifth, and sixth houses are hit with hard aspects). This is the home team's lower half of the chart.

At times you may get an even distribution concerning the upper and lower half of the chart. Until you gain more experience in working with event charts that are set up for the time and location of the home team, you should avoid betting on even distributions of angular house cusps and their rulers. However, if you wish to give it a try consider the team that has more aspects to planets either in the forth or tenth houses. If there are more aspects involving the fourth house or its ruler, it would naturally indicate the home team as the winner. If there are more aspects involving the tenth house or its ruler, it would naturally indicate that the visiting team would be the winner.

The more games you do, the better. Gradually through experience and research in working with game charts you'll soon be getting ninety percent of your teams correct. The other ten percent will be due to human error.